LADDERS INTERVIEWS GUIDE
2020 Edition

Marc Cenedella

www.theladders.com
@LaddersHQ

LADDERS

Marc Cenedella: Founder and CEO

ISBN: 978-1-7337627-4-8

Contents

1. Introduction to Ladders Interviews Guide 5

2. Before the interview 17

3. During the interview: 49 questions they'll ask you 45

4. During the interview: 25 questions you'll ask them 91

5. After the interview: Saying thank you 113

More best practices & advice online 121

About the Author 123

1. INTRODUCTION TO LADDERS INTERVIEWS GUIDE

It was a surprisingly warm day for February when I bombed my interview.

Arriving at the promising, sky-rocketing internet company, I chilled out in the cool loft lobby. The seats weren't comfortable, but they looked expensive. I fidgeted with my Blackberry, turning the scroll wheel with my thumb, each turn giving off a satisfying click that reminded me I was living in the future. And you know what? Once I nailed the interview and got this job, I would actually be creating the future!

It was 1999, and the enormous tidal wave of internet interest had washed over all of America. I wanted to be a part of it. I needed to be a part of it. I'd been a computer geek in junior high, but lost interest when the college courses turned out to be actually very hard, while the output remained pretty obscure and remote from daily life. I'd stayed interested though, and this amazing sweep of new technology promising to change our daily lives attracted me immensely.

And oh! The parties! I'd gone last night to another of the internet bashes — extravagant, exorbitant, exotic beacons of the future coming our way. And maybe a hangover, too, seemed to be coming my way. I'd had to skip breakfast to make this morning interview, but it was all in service of my bright future, and I was a willing, thrilling participant in it all.

In this new job, I'd be pushing boundaries, thinking outside the box, and making other cliches come to life. It was remarkable — only two years out of business school and all of this was happening for me **right now**. In real life.

Amazing!

Excitement, adrenaline, and the drumbeat of internet riches pumped through my head. My interviewer, the Chief Officer of… I'm not quite sure what department… had appeared in the lobby and was walking me through the strange blend of expensive wall art and dumpy corridors that internet companies in New York were known for. The enormous conference room had the musky scent of Early Internet — recently-installed drywall, computers baking in a nearby closet, and an old steam pipe exposed at the edge of the room beneath huge windows. This converted loft in SoHo was exactly the cool place I'd been reading about in edgy internet (print) magazines.

Man, I was excited!

The Chief Something Officer opened the conversation with "Tell me about yourself" and I… *froze.*

And by froze, I mean I seized up, ground to a halt, felt the white hot heat creeping up my neck, which was shortly followed by a warm red wave of embarrassment flowing from the top of my head. I froze, I choked, I blanked. No words, no sounds, would come out. It was the flop sweats. The yips. The big choke.

I somehow managed to convey that I'd had the flu and that it must be overcoming me, as I picked up my things to get out of the dumpy room in the beautiful loft in the fancy part of Manhattan. If it had been possible to invisibly convey myself down the dumpy corridor— to pass unseen through doors, walls, and lobby in order to get to the elevators — I was going to make the attempt.

But I'm pretty sure they saw me all the way out.

I'd choked! All my dreams of internet riches, and inventing the future, and helping create the Internet… gone! I was horrified. Appalled. Embarrassed. Ashamed. I'd graduated with honors from America's top business school just two years ago on the strength of my in-class participation. I'd done dozens, probably hundreds, of interviews. And while I always got a little keyed up beforehand — butterflies in the stomach and all that — I'd managed to pull it together and roll along rather well once things got going, thankyouverymuch. I'd frozen like a puddle in the Buffalo winter.

And yet... something in that appalling experience touched me, and eventually propelled me into becoming America's leading career advice author. I was transfixed by the power of it, the business drama of the interview and its consequences.

Job interviews, it struck me, are highly-charged events with lots of emotion, tons at stake, and a direct influence on an outcome of great significance to all involved. Job interviews have an extraordinary variety of participants, with wildly unpredictable styles and behaviors. They happen frequently enough that you ought to study for them, but infrequently enough that it's difficult to stay in good practice. Outside of dating, there is no conversation as meaningful for one's destiny, no stressful event that Americans volunteer for as often, with such dramatic crashes, victories, humbling and heroic outcomes, as the job interview.

This book is for people who choke on interviews, and for people who don't choke on interviews. It's for those who blather on and on, those who fail to answer the question, and those who don't get the joke. It's for those who are confident, those who are overconfident, and those who aren't confident at all. It's for the clever and the uncertain, the capable and the confused. It's for those who get asked impossible brain teasers, and those who prefer brain teasers to talking about themselves. It's for those who remember the title of the job for which they're interviewing, and those who hope the interviewer reminds them.

This book, in short, is for all American professionals who have been on a job interview and will be again. And it's especially written with a long-ago thirtysomething MBA in New York City in mind, who really wished he'd had this book to read before heading into an interview with that cool, cool, internet company in a SoHo loft. Because over the next 90 minutes, you'll learn how everything I did wrong that day back in February 1999 set me up to fail — the lack of sleep, the hangover, the lack of preparation, not understanding the company or its business, not even knowing with whom I was interviewing — all made a lousy performance likely, perhaps even inevitable.

The advice in this book is targeted to professionals with 10+ years experience, and is written with those examples and situations in mind. But unlike other books in Ladders' Guide series, the advice given here is broadly applicable to any professional interviewing for any white-collar job, from intern to vice chairwoman.

I like to write "how come" guides, not just "how to" guides. It's a different approach from other career writers, who start their interview pointers with dress code choices and a long list of interview questions. Over two decades of giving advice, I've found that professionals like you are more powerful when they understand the "why" first.

When you understand your goals in an interview, and the goals of the interviewers, you're better able to put advice into practice. Addressing your interviewer's goals, rather than your own, your answers will resonate more effectively, your interviews will be more compelling, more productive, and lead to more relevant and valuable job offers.

Understanding why your interviewer seems so ill-prepared, keeps asking you about the job you did rather than the job you want to do, and seems genuinely surprised when you have questions for him, will all help you master the "how come" of interviews. And when you've mastered that, performing the "how to" becomes much easier.

In about 90 minutes, I'll give you what you need to know to perform your best in a job interview. That's all the time you need to learn the basics of interviewing — your time is valuable, so I've only made room for the most important stuff. If, when you're done, you still have an appetite for more, we host a page with more interview questions, advice and information here: **www.theladders.com/career-advice/interviews-guide** .

The goals of interviewing

In interviews, your four goals are:

1. To share the truth about working with you.
2. To determine if there's a fit with the roles you're considering.
3. To be better prepared for your next interview.
4. To generate job offers for you.

Let's take each of these in order.

The **first goal of interviews** is to provide a true and compelling picture of you and your capabilities to a potential future boss and interviewing team. While it is a special version of you that shows up for an interview — more practiced, more rehearsed, more polished, more aware of the impact of every word, better able to keep your bad habits or sloppy tendencies in check — your goal is to present your performance capabilities, personal preferences, and working style accurately.

The **second goal of interviews** is for you and your future boss to determine if this role is the right fit for you. You both have an opinion, you both have requirements, you both get a vote. By comparing your mutual needs, capabilities, and desires, your hope is to discover if there's a match. Sometimes this will mean, in the end, that you don't want the job. Other times, that you don't get the job.

Thank goodness! You're seeking the right match, not any match, and mutual truth-telling in a well-run interview process aids that objective.

The **third goal for interviews** is preparation. Interviews are becoming more frequent. The rise of the internet, a more flexible workforce, and shorter job tenure, all mean that you'll be coming into contact with HR groups and recruiters more often. When you do, they might behave nothing like they did the last time around. I'll share with you the latest trends and fads in interviewing. While circular in reasoning, part of the goal of interviews is to get better at doing interviews.

We'll also discuss the right amount of preparation for each in-person, phone, videoconference, or remote interview. The right amount of preparation will leave you feeling enthusiastic before the interview, help you maintain a good rapport with your interviewer, and arm you with the questions appropriate to your role and level. You'll avoid being over-prepared or over-scripted, which can harm your job interview performance as much as being under-prepared.

The fourth, and supreme, goal of interviews is to generate job offers. Specifically, offers of employment for jobs that you can succeed in, that advance your career in exchange for compensation that is attractive to you. Whether or not you eventually decide to take that offer is a separate decision, but the goal of interviewing is to have a company, firm, or organization extend to you an offer of employment for your consideration.

At the core of my advice is knowing the three things your future boss wants from the open role for which you are interviewing. It's deceptively simple, and deceptively effective. Too often, interviewers are undisciplined, allowing conversation to wander across a wide-open field of agreeable topics, with time running out before the most relevant questions are addressed. We want to make sure you get your points across effectively, and have the time to ask the questions most important to you.

We'll discuss how to ask each interviewer for the three criteria most important to success in a role. I'll encourage you to ask each interviewer this same question, and observe what you learn by comparing their answers. At its simplest level, this question uncovers their highest needs and enables you to share your capabilities in those areas. By asking the HR person or recruiter, and each interviewer, at the start of each conversation, to tell you the three most important factors for success in this role, they will... reveal their priorities to you. It's so easy, it seems unfair — they're giving you the answers before the test gets started!

We'll discuss the most under-appreciated interview skill — listening — and how you can use it to get ahead in interviews. How you ask questions, and which questions you ask, communicate as much about how you think and how you collaborate as your answers. You should never run out of questions with an interviewer, only the time to ask them. Using your question time wisely greatly improves your performance.

An additional goal of interviewing is to provide lifestyle insurance for you and your family. You ought to be consistently interviewing throughout your career. There may be no better way to secure your peace of mind, learn your options in a downturn, and raise your awareness of how economic conditions may or may not impact you, than by regularly interviewing at a consistent pace for jobs outside your present role. 2020 seems to be a very strong year economically — the best we've seen since the 1960s in fact — and opportunities to interview abound. It is a great time to get into the very good habit of interviewing for practice. That way you will be prepared when downturns come in the years ahead.

We'll discuss managing "jitters," "nerves," and "butterflies in your stomach." These feelings and emotions are real and get in the way of good interview performance. Sometimes, the anxiety we feel in interviews can overwhelm and derail us, as it did me at the beginning of this chapter. The sweaty palms, panicky brain, and stammering answers that occur on our worst days simply come from a lack of familiarity with interviewing.

We'll discuss in detail how to conquer your nerves by improving your knowledge. The more you understand the goals, practices, and behaviors of everyone involved in interviewing, the more you'll realize that it's not such a mysterious process. In fact, everyone involved is usually under-trained and under-prepared. The more familiar you are with interviews, the better you'll be able to steer situations to your desired outcome.

I'll also nudge you repeatedly to take care of yourself, managing your biology, psychology and travel time to ensure your best performance. We want the sweaty hands and heightened anxiety of interviews to turn into the applause of being welcomed at your new job on your first day of work.

Now, of course, **the best way to interview well is to perform well**. Great performance in your current job makes for great interviews: you'll have the best stories, accomplishments and achievements to share. In the boardroom, it's said that great numbers make for great meetings. In the job search, it's great results that make for great interviews.

Sometimes, interviews result in not getting the offer you desired, or not accepting the offer they extended. In the short run, this feels like defeat — a waste of time, a waste of effort, a waste of hope and enthusiasm. But it is far better for negative feedback to occur now than in your performance reviews over the years to come. Discovering a mismatch before you start allows an easy fix — don't take the job. Fixing a bad match once you're inside a company is much, much harder on you, and your future boss. Sometimes "no" is the best outcome, and you should realize that it is a *successful* outcome, even if bittersweet.

I'll cap my advice with how to put a cherry on top. The steps you take after an interview rarely determine the outcome, but can build on the positive momentum you've created in the interview room. Using your post-interview "thank you" to re-emphasize your three selling points is the smart, effective way to leverage your time together into the beginnings of a meaningful working relationship.

Interviews are consequential, wondrous moments in the lives of American professionals. Sometimes the results are fortunate even when the outcome is bad. The interview I bombed, as it turns out, was for a company on its way to flaming out eighteen months later. And the bracing reminder of that experience caused me to prepare much more effectively for my next interview, at one of America's leading job companies, where I accepted a role that catapulted me into my present career. Having written America's largest career advice newsletter for the past 15 years, I'd like to share with you what I've learned about making your interviews effective.

The results, two decades later, are in the pages ahead.

Let's get started…

2. BEFORE THE INTERVIEW

Cavemen didn't interview.

There were no interviews on the savannah: "Say, Og, we're a tribe of hunter-gatherers between pastures and we're looking to add a gatherer to our clan. Can you tell me about your experience in berries?"

Many of the features of modern social life — and even work life — were present back there on the savannah: friends, family, likes and dislikes, peer pressure, dating, and even working together for the hunt or harvest. But no interviews.

There are no interviews in the Bible, either. You'll look in vain for the Apostles or the Maccabees being asked for references, or quizzed on the annual volume of water flowing through the Nile.

George Washington didn't interview for his job; he actually ducked out of the room entirely when John Adams brought up his name in Congress as the perfect candidate for Commander-in-Chief.

From cavemen until about the time of the Civil War, in fact, your ancestors didn't have jobs and didn't go on job interviews. Instead, your folks in the "Old Country" grew up, lived, and worked within 10 miles of where they were born. Almost everyone they met was from their own tribe. And like everybody else, they worked for the king, the church, the army, or, most likely, were farmers, serfs, or slaves.

As late as 1860, farmers made up two-thirds of the U.S. workforce. It was only after the Civil War and the rise of industrialization that enormous new factories producing steel, shoes, railroad cars, or pork bellies, rose up across the country. It was these entirely new institutions that created what we've come to think of as "a job."

Statistically, then, it was not until your great-grandparents' time that your forebears started going on job interviews. They most likely did "blue-collar" interviews for manual and physical work — tests of their ability to hold a shovel or pull a lever, an assessment of their likelihood to show up on time and sober, and a confirmation of their ability to follow English language instructions. Coming from their small world "down on the farm" where they knew the butcher, the baker, and the candlestick maker, to a world with hundreds or thousands of potential bosses and coworkers, was a change in scale and scope as terrifying as it was exhilarating.

For most professional Americans, their parents were the first generation in their family who went on "white-collar" interviews: facing questions about teamwork, diligence, abstract reasoning, college preparation, and the odd brain teaser. Immediately after World War II, the interview process tended to resemble a combination of army life and social club admissions — a very impersonal, detached, almost clinical measurement of the man, along with some discreet inquiries into who you were related to and where your family was from.

Today's American workplace, by contrast, is a bewildering world in which startups run by college kids are more prestigious than century-old names. The familiar hierarchies of the past had the oldest, wisest, most respected people at the top of the pyramid, not some scrawny geeks. In recent decades, the disruption of old companies, old manners, and old loyalties, and the rise of a very fast-paced modern American workplace confuses and confounds many of our social cues, expectations, and tribal mores. All of which upends our expectations, and our standing, in the social circles that make up human life.

This very brief history lesson is a prelude to a central point of *Ladders Interviews Guide, 2020 Edition*: interviews aren't normal for humans. They're not normal for human psychology or physiology. They're not normal for humans' social expectations. They weren't a normal feature of any human society, anywhere on the planet, prior to about 100 years ago. They are deeply strange experiences for a wide variety of reasons; the sooner you understand that any and all of your anxieties about interviews come from your biology, anthropology, physiology and genealogy, and none are because you are "bad" at interviewing, the sooner you and I can take productive steps to make you "interview anxiety proof." So stick with me.

We humans developed, as a species, in small tribes back on that savannah. For most of our time on earth, it's been easy to separate other humans into camps of friend or foe. Among the friends, we had only two categories: close family or distant family. Among foes, the only distinction that mattered was "dead or alive." And the social interactions we are familiar with — sucking up to the top ape, joshing with the other fellas and gals in the pack, finding our place in the pecking order — have their roots in this time when we lived in small tribes.

For almost our entire existence as a species, unfamiliar strangers were dangerous, not potential future coworkers. Strangers provoked anxiety, uncertainty and confusion, not excitement about potentially working together. There was no need to make introductions or small talk with people you didn't know, because everyone you knew, knew you back in return. A small, boxy room full of strangers, or even a single stranger, triggered the "fight or flight" response — our primordial safety mechanism that kept us from getting killed before we got back to the campfire.

Of course, humans do a lot of things in the modern world that we didn't do back then. If we can get comfortable with very unnatural activities such as skydiving, taking elevators, or riding a bike, surely we can adjust to interviewing? But humans adjust to some changes better than others. When it comes to **technological** change — picking up new tools, technology gadgets, or other material things — we pick up expertise pretty fast and get comfortable with daily use amazingly quickly.

But when it comes to interactions with other humans, we primarily learn how to handle these by mimicking the behavior we see from parents and peers. The right way to behave, what to expect when having a conversation, what's acceptable and not acceptable when talking to strangers, how to present yourself to peers — all come from social learning. You try something out, and then your parents, who were taught by their parents, who were taught by their parents, correct you and teach you what to expect.

So how to act at a dinner, while playing sports, on the hunt, while farming in the garden, with your kids, or in a war — all of these have been taught, and handed down, for generations immemorial.

Interviews combine an important event that has far-reaching outcomes, with little understanding of what should be expected. And that is a marvelous recipe for performance anxiety. Indeed, for almost all of human history, feeling nervous — or alarmed! — was the correct response when confronted by a stranger in a small room peppering you with questions. It was almost always a telling sign that you were in danger. "Get Out!" exclaimed the title of the 2018 Oscar winning movie on just this theme of the danger of those outside your tribe.

As a result, without a common social understanding to refer to, it's difficult to know how to feel about the interview process:

The interview went long — *is that good or bad?*

They haven't called back in four days — *is that good or bad?*

They've asked me in for a fourth round of interviews to meet more people — *is that good or bad?*

Interviews are not normal for humans. They are awkward, unusual, and uncomfortable. As a result, your anxiety is normal... expected, even. It's not an accident, it's not just you, it's not that you have a uniquely bad reaction to interviews. The truth of the matter is that the nature of interviewing is so unlike anything else we do in our lives, or that our families did in their lives, that extreme discomfort should be considered the normal reaction. Even the most successful, most powerful, people I've helped over the years feel nervous and self-conscious about interviews, especially when they're out of practice. Until you've personally done several hundred interviews on either side of the table, anxiety and nerves will be a part of the process for you. So it's more than just common, it's universal. You'll need to manage it, not hope you can wish it away.

Three most important things

An interview should answer whether you are right for the hiring firm, the role, and your future boss. What are her specific needs from the role? Is there a particular style in which she is looking to have the work done? Do you match up with the title, pay, skills, role, span of control, prior experience, capabilities, communication style, and work cadence that your boss expects for the role? Ensuring, to the greatest extent possible, that there is a match between your qualities, and her desires, is half of the battle.

The other half is determining if the firm is right for you. Interviews are absolutely not one-way streets, and too often candidates allow their questions to be afterthoughts. Does the role make sense as a logical next step on your career path? Does it match up with your ambitions and direction? Does the company meet your desires on company size, culture, and pace?

These are obvious questions, yet they are often left unanswered in the dramatic whirlwind of interviewing courtship. I have counseled otherwise bright and capable professionals who were romanced through a recruiting process to take a job entirely outside of their interests or plans. There's a reason so many new hires don't work out, and the "swept off your feet" interview process is a culprit. I'd guess that, by 20 years into their careers, most American professionals have at least one *mulligan* job. Has it ever happened to you? If not, you're stronger than most.

To best determine your ability to do what the role takes: **ask**. It's advice so simple as to barely qualify as advice, were it not for the hundreds of times I've asked people going to interviews, "What are the most important things they're looking for from the role?" only to be met with a blank stare or a mumble.

So… ask.

When you're setting up the interview, ask the HR person, recruiter or hiring manager: **"Which three things are most important to success in this role?"** You only want to know three, because that'll be about the number of factors you'll be able to manage throughout multiple days of interviews. It also forces prioritization on their part. Sure, there are dozens of things they'd like from this hire, but indicating which are the three **most** important reveals their thinking. Further, whether it's reviewing your work history in the context of these three items, comparing the varying answers from interviewers, or confirming with the boss after your interview that she heard your points loud and clear — three is a magic number for making a strong case.

It may not surprise you to know that the company will gladly tell you which three things are most important to success in the job. They'll be pleasantly surprised you asked. Because so few people start off the interview process by focusing on the company's needs rather than their own abilities, you'll stand out from the start. It's an encouraging sign to the interviewers that your style is to understand them better, before talking about yourself.

When the HR person or recruiter provides you with the three most important factors, you should do a careful review. Do these three performance factors match up with your strengths and what you're looking to do next? If all three are right on target, that's terrific, and you'll be prepared to nail each interview thoroughly.

Conversely, if all three are completely off the mark, your course of action is simple — you let the recruiter know there isn't a fit, because your background or career path doesn't match up. You may be tempted to fudge a bit, on the theory that getting your foot in the door is better than no interview at all, but this is not a productive approach. Informing the company and HR team upfront of the mismatch impresses with your self-awareness, your respect for their time, and your good judgment. By showing your good manners as a candidate, you're **more** likely to be made aware of other opportunities, not less. Especially if you position your feedback as, "I'm not right for that role because of reasons one, two and three, but if you have something come open that requires x, y and z, I'd be a better candidate for that kind of opportunity," you are setting yourself up for success by communicating proactively and clearly.

The trouble comes if there is a mix among the three factors — one or two of the three do not match up, while the others do line up with your background or interests. In these cases, it's your business judgment as to whether and how hard to pursue. Raise these issues with the HR person or recruiter prior to heading in for the interview. It could be that they've misstated their priorities, and will clarify for you in a way that makes a go / no-go decision easier. But, ultimately, the call will be yours as to whether or not proceeding is a good use of your time, and theirs.

Preparation and Research

Allocate one hour of preparation time for each hour of interview time. This will strike you as an impossible burden at first, and a pile of additional work on top of an already packed day. But like the saying about restaurants — "if you can't afford the tip, you can't afford the restaurant" — **if you don't have the time to prepare, you don't have the time to interview**.

To put it into perspective, if you get 10 relevant interview opportunities, half will last one hour total, and the other half will last four hours over two rounds, not including travel time. That's 25 hours of interviewing. Adding 25 hours of prep time is the right amount. Investing 50 to 100 hours, every three or four years, to maximize your professional satisfaction and compensation, may be an investment you will come to believe is justified. It certainly underscores that finding a new job is, in itself, a full-time job.

You should do the "right" amount of research for the interview, neither under-preparing nor over-preparing. This means showing up with a "good" level of knowledge after doing a "reasonable" amount of research.

On one hand, there is the distressing number of professionals, at mid- and even senior levels, who show up for an interview without even visiting the company's website. We all get it — time is tight and you're busy. But allowing crunch time to eliminate your preparation is foolish and you'll look bad.

On the other hand, there are the people who overdo it and show up with eight pages of single-spaced questions. They start the interview by asking why margins in the Southwest European region have declined by 10% over the past seven years despite favorable currency rates. Candidates such as these do seem to have missed the point of an in-person, human-to-human connection.

The questions you raise, and the research you bring, reveal something about your business judgment. "Right" is in the eye of the beholder. Are your questions reasonably related to the job? Your duties? Or are you asking simply to show off, or play trivia games? Your approach reveals something meaningful about how you handle meetings, conversations, and business tasks. Your actions speak much louder than your words, so be clear about the message you'd like to send with your preparation and questions.

Similarly, you'd like to know a reasonable amount about your interviewers before interviewing with them. Clarify ahead of time with the HR person or recruiter: What is the day going to be like? How long will interviews last? Is it one long interview or a few that are broken up? Who are the interviewers I'll be meeting with? Is there anything in particular they like candidates to prepare in advance? What questions will they typically ask? (This last question is a bit cheeky, but you never know — sometimes the junior HR person will pass you this very valuable information!) Is there anything else I can or should prepare?

With this information, do a modest amount of research on your interviewer — a couple facts, a few recent press mentions, her latest shares on Twitter or blog posts on industry-related subject matter. Don't overdo the research on your interviewer's background. Mentioning where the interviewer's spouse went to college, or asking about an obscure media appearance several years back, is creepy, not impressive. It's easy to overdo this, so don't.

If you can't determine the names of each person interviewing you, or the HR people are being coy, the best you can do is learn something about the department and what they're up to. Have they been expanding, taking on new tasks, producing something in the public eye? Your goal is to show sufficient interest to have done some research, but not enough to show obsession.

All these matters are cases of business judgment, and you need to calibrate for your level, role, and place in the industry. You can draw on your experiences with candidates that seemed unprepared or over-prepared, or discuss with peers and former colleagues what's appropriate. Your good questions will display interest, capability, gravitas, and curiosity.

To take an example, the $100,000 / year manager in marketing is expected to know the kind of marketing a company is doing, to have observed it in the wild in a few places, and to have a sense of the process by which it was produced. Relevant questions could include why the firm chose those channels, and how pleased they were with the agencies assisting them.

The $450,000 / year CMO, on the other hand, brings an assessment of different channels and their efficacy for the company's purposes, a high-level appraisal of the quality of the creative currently flighted, potential avenues for improving it, and a viewpoint on channel prioritization. His questions might focus on the business objectives intended, the outcomes of the company's current marketing efforts, why they've tried what they've tried so far, what was off the table or a sacred cow, and questions about the trade-off between goosing sales and building the brand long-term.

Visiting the company's website is surprisingly overlooked. Spend 15 minutes of your preparation time reviewing their website, as well as other online resources, to gain a summary understanding of the company's current efforts, perceptions, and results.

For easy reference, here's a list you can follow, which is also available at **https://www.theladders.com/career-advice/interviews-guide** :

- Read three of the latest articles at Google News when doing a search for the company's name.
- If a public company, read the Morningstar, Bloomberg, or MarketWatch entry on the company.
- Read the company's Wikipedia entry.

- There's the old joke that a company's org chart is reflected in their website navigation, and I've found this to be surprisingly (and alarmingly) true. It will be helpful for you to read through the four to six top-level navigation items on the company site, usually including "About Us," "Products/ Services," "Our (Executive) Team," "Clients / Customers," and "News / Press". It also makes sense to view the "Careers" tab of the company to see what other roles they're hiring and if that indicates anything meaningful to you.

- Do they have Facebook, Twitter, Instagram links on their homepage? Most companies do. If so, follow each one and take brief notes on what you see in the first four photos, posts, or tweets. If not, then that in itself is a good topic to raise with your interviewer ("I see you've chosen not to have a social media presence — how did you reach the conclusion that that was right for the company?")

- Visit the company's page on Ladders, where we have collected much of the above information for you: **https://www.theladders.com/company-search**

Try to keep this web surfing exercise to just 15 minutes. It's easy to spend all of your preparation time clicking around the internet if you're not careful. Fifteen minutes gives you a good level of knowledge, and allows you to preserve the other 45 minutes for thinking through your approach and your answers in detail.

During this web review, it's extremely helpful if you can write down three to four company-specific questions that you can ask during your interview. They don't need to be deep or profound, but they do need to be related specifically to the company. A few high-level "why" questions about the new product launch, a new role they're hiring for outside of your field, a new hire, or an old rivalry with a competitor, all fit the bill. We'll dig into your side of the two-way interview street in detail in Section 4, so for now the important thing is to write down a few questions that show you've done the basic research.

Prepare your mind

As you approach your interview, **be nice**. It's good advice every day, but it's especially important in the context of your interview. Be nice to the people arranging your time with the company. They're typically young people doing a thankless job, negotiating scheduling difficulties and circumstances beyond their control, for dozens or hundreds of candidates at the same time. A word of kindness can work wonders for you. A snarl or a curt response can cause problems.

When you get to the building, **be nice** to the receptionist. Southwest Airlines was the pioneer in asking receptionists to report on candidate behavior, and your first interactions count. Modern interview and candidate management software makes it very easy for anybody in the company to give blunt "Yelp-style" feedback on you. It's surprising to discover the number of people who think good manners and pleasantness need only to be trotted out in the interview room. Don't accidentally fall into this category. You should be kind to every employee you meet. Truth be told, you should be kind to everybody within two miles of the interview — the receptionist, the parking lot guy, the janitor and the intern. For extra credit, practice this kindness even when you're not interviewing — it might be good advice in general for someone at your professional level.

Please be aware that interviews are subject to forces beyond the company's control. Some, or all, of the plan for the day could go out the window before you even set foot in the building. When you arrive, ask the HR person or recruiter about their experience with how much give-and-take is in the day's schedule, giving you another chance to probe the specific expectations for your interviews. Is the schedule typically set in stone and run on a tight schedule, or is there wide latitude in the day? Will the interviewers vary in their questions, or do they all tend to ask the same set? Do they ask surprise or difficult questions on purpose? Is there a formal review after the interview, or is it handled more informally? Should things go well, how does it progress after this stage?

It's good to get in the habit of taking notes. You'll never remember who said what as you sit down to write thank you notes days later. If, like me, you're challenged in the note-taking department, start the interview with "1. 2. 3." written on the top of an otherwise blank piece of paper and you might feel some compulsion to take a trio of notes for later reference.

Finally, make time to put yourself into a positive and productive state of mind. What gets your drive going? Music is a common one — Early Dylan? Late Dead? Electronica, Bieber, or that Katy Perry song from a couple summers back? Or are there readings that calm, inspire, energize you? Photos that remind you of special people, special times, special places? Videos of wingsuits that make you scream, classic movie scenes that go gunga-ga-lunga, a miracle on ice that makes you cheer every time?

Whatever it is, turn it on, turn it up, and tune yourself in to be your best.

Prepare and manage your body

You'll want to have a pre-interview routine that covers your biology and psychology — what do you need to eat and drink? How often do you need to go to the restroom? How are you dressed? How much space in your schedule are you going to give yourself to arrive on time?

Now, when I suggest that you need to think about handling bathroom breaks, or ask if you're wearing a warm enough coat, or if you've eaten enough for breakfast, you'll say I sound like your grandmother. And sure, you do all these things in your life without much input from me, so why should that change now?

There's a good answer.

The reason you need to explicitly think through the basics is that none of the basics are taken care of for you on interview days. You're going to strange buildings, in strange locations, with unfamiliar arrangements for bathrooms, heaters, air conditioning, cafes and vending machines. You don't want to be going through caffeine withdrawal in an interview only to discover the only Starbucks is two miles away across the corporate campus.

You are familiar with your own biology, having cohabitated with your body, lo these many years, but it's good to remind yourself of your biological limits ahead of your interviews. Do you need bio breaks often, or not? Does that vary in response to coffee and water consumption? Are there other triggers you need to be mindful of? When I was coming out of business school and interviewing around Manhattan, I ended up with an extensive and specific understanding of hotel restrooms I could duck into as I roamed midtown. My favorite is still

The Peninsula Hotel, second floor past the reception desk — always immaculate!

For beverages, how do you perform best? Are you fine living off the land — you'll take water if that's all they have — or is there a specific make, mix, or *macchiato* that you need to ingest to survive the day? Will you pick it up there, or are you bringing it with you?

If the interviews are early in the morning, over lunch hour, during dinner time, or scheduled to last more than four hours, how are you going to manage hunger? The interview process itself can be incredibly taxing, so you don't want to add calorie starvation or low blood sugar on top of interview stress. The simplest solution is to have two snack bars or their equivalent in your backpack or purse. My current favorite is the RxBar, Chocolate Sea Salt. Whatever yours might be, you should acquire a box to keep at the office.

Are you dressing warm enough, cool enough, with comfortable shoes, in a shirt or blouse that fits or flatters? If you're in sales, this is of course old hat to you. But if you're an engineer, or accountant, there's a reasonable chance you actually haven't thought about this in a while, have you?

Are you dressing business casual? Casual casual? Business attire? The advice for interview dress has changed substantially in the past five years. It's no longer the case that you should default to coat and tie, or pearls and heels, for a job interview. Even the CEOs of 7 out of 10 of America's most valuable companies go without a necktie (unless they're getting an award or shaking a President's hand), so the perception of what's appropriate has moved dramatically toward the casual. The higher you go in your career, the more scrutinized your appearance will be, so it merits your attention.

It's advisable to check-in with the HR person on dress code. If they provide a wishy-washy answer, please press them a little bit: Is half the office wearing ties? Is half the office wearing flip-flops? What will my interviewers be wearing? If they're vague, you can always ask, "Will I feel out of place in a coat and tie / string of pearls and heels?" — if they answer "not at all," you know it's expected.

Smart business casual with nice shoes is probably going to be the dress code for most interviews these days. The old advice, that you could almost never go wrong with a tie, is no longer true. Today the advice is: **dress upscale, not out of scale.** Over-dressing for an interview can send negative cues to your future coworkers at a more casual workplace. They may make conclusions about your ability to read and understand their environment. Subconsciously, they question whether you could really be "one of us." If, conversely, you need to step it up a notch or two in professionalism, make sure you "break in" your new attire with a couple of trial runs to ensure fit and comfort.

And in the cases where you just don't get the memo ahead of time, and there's a disastrous clash between your look and the office habitat, be prepared to laugh it off. It happens.

Keep the cologne or perfume to a sliver. I've never heard of someone hired for their wonderful and powerful aroma, but plenty of horror stories the other way.

What time are you going to bring yourself to the interview? 12 minutes before the first interview is the perfect time to arrive for an interview in America in 2020 — that's early enough to be early, without being a burden on your first meeting. To arrive twelve minutes early, your initial departure time depends on what's realistic with your current work, how manageable or unmanageable the commute may be, and what Google Maps or Waze say about the length of time required for travel. If you've not been late to a meeting in the past decade, then you don't need my assistance — for the rest of us, it bears careful thought. By the way, did you double-confirm the address with a live human being, such as the HR person, rather than rely on the occasionally out-of-date Google Maps? And have you put the address in the calendar invite on your smartphone?

You should show up on-time, unflustered, with a half-dozen clean, well-presented copies of your resume printed out on paper. Plain ol' white paper is fine in 2020. There is no need for the ivory-colored cream paper that your great aunt bought you for graduation. Because you'll take notes, you should bring your favorite pad and writing implement. If you need visuals or a portfolio, you should have that ready to go on your tablet or laptop. If you've written out your questions, you should have them printed on paper in case your phone or laptop dies on you.

And for every time you might be snickering at me for proffering such miniscule advice on these terrifically trivial matters, I can point you toward an experienced professional who casually mis-estimated, mis-timed, or misunderstood his planning, and suffered through a poor interview as a result. If you end up being well-prepared for all your interviews, while chortling at my henpecking, I will be a pleased career advice author, and won't mind your teasing at all!

The final step before we head to the interview itself is for you to consider your purpose and your goals.

Why are you interviewing?

Boredom, curiosity, a need to move on, ambition, growth, learning, a defensive move, insurance in troubled times? What are your reasons for interviewing? And what do you want from this interview in particular? Are you hoping to get practice at interviewing, compliments, praise, an offer, a very attractive offer, a way out, competitive information, a validation? For the purposes of this book, it's useful for you to think through what you desire in your career as a next step — is it money, title, power, responsibility, glory, recognition, a bigger platform or more intimacy, a different role / industry / angle on the problems you've worked on before? To quote Joe Jackson, "You can't get what you want, till you know what you want."

Now, inevitably, you'll find yourself stumbling into an interview without having reflected as to whether or not you're truly available. It could be a variety of circumstances — a casual advisory role suddenly turns serious, an industry luminary flatters you into her office and a compensation discussion, a bad day leads to a kind word from a recruiter leads to a third round of interviewing before you know it. There's a degree to which interviewing is healthy in an economic system without loyalty, such as ours; but that requires you to understand that you always have the power, and the obligation, to say "no thanks" to the wrong opportunities regardless of the compliments strewn in your path.

Additionally, an interview is not a judgment on you as a human being, or even as a business professional. One interview, or several, cannot pass meaningful judgment on you as a person, your value as a professional, your place on the planet, or whether you should feel good or bad about yourself today. An interview is a tool a company uses for making a judgment as to whether you're right for a role, and the role is right for you. As much as it stings, you can't take unsuccessful interviews as a meaningful review of your worth, value or professionalism. It's just not what they are designed to do.

Interviews are also not meant to belittle you, but occasionally, that's what they'll do. Often, hopefully most of the time, your race, gender, and age (be it young or old), won't impact your ability to get the job. I wish it were all the time, but that's just not true. When these non-business factors intrude on your interview, you'll need to make a fast decision about the kind of culture you can live with. It's not fair, it's not right, and it's not moral, but there are few effective adjustments you can make to deal with the failings in your fellow man. Solving the societal problems involved is beyond the scope of this book, so we will sidestep them in this guide and target our efforts for a better world to a different venue.

Showing up for the interview is, not surprisingly, an important part of succeeding at the interview. Don't take yourself out of the running before you've even started. After persuading an audience member at one of my talks to go through with his interviews, he sent me a follow up note:

> *"We met briefly at last Wednesday's Yale Tech meetup. I was the one so nervous about a Friday interview that I was considering taking myself out of the running.*
>
> *"Nerves notwithstanding, on your encouragement and the encouragement of many others, I headed in for a full day of interviews on Friday. Long story short, I came home to find an offer in my email! It's a huge step forward in my career and is honestly more than I'd hoped for when I started looking around.*
>
> *"So, I just want to say thank you very much for the helpful words. They made a difference, and I'm going to be feeling that difference for years to come.*
>
> *"Best..."*

Overcoming a case of nerves is essential to overcoming the obstacles to your career progression. I know the absurdity of job interviews, your own self-doubts, and mistaken cues you interpret from the recruiter… all of these conspire to encourage surrender without a fight. Faced with dangerous, or uncomfortable, situations, you'll find reasons to avoid them — it's that old "fight or flight" response. You may come up with a variety of ways to talk yourself out of going to an interview — that you're not good enough, or that surely there are better candidates among the competition, or that something the HR person said could be a secret hint that they're not really interested.

Shakespeare, as usual, may have said it best: "Our doubts are traitors, and make us lose the good we oft might win, by fearing to attempt."

These traitors, seemingly powerful doubts that help you rationalize why it's a better use of your time to **not** pursue the opportunity, are just the normal anxiety of the job search getting the best of you. Faced with new situations and high stakes, we look too eagerly for clues to escape, and settle too readily on dubious answers. You can safely ignore almost all of the guesses you make about how the interview process might be playing out, and what interviewers might or might not be thinking about you — they're usually inaccurate, misleading, and ineffective signals as to your actual chances. It's far better to stick with your plan, follow through on your interviews and give yourself a chance to get ahead.

3. DURING THE INTERVIEW: 49 QUESTIONS THEY'LL ASK YOU

They've asked you to "wait right here for just a bit" and now it's 15 minutes past the time your next interview was supposed to start and you're trying to read the tea leaves. Does that mean they're just putting the finishing touches on their generous offer? Or have they changed their mind and want to figure out how to let me down gently? Maybe they've found something they love on my resume? Or maybe something they hate? What should I do? You hands are sweating, you're uptight, and this big interview hasn't even started!

Of course, unbeknownst to you, the reason your interviewer is late is because the mechanic down at the garage has lost her credit card number (again) and she's patiently repeating it for him over the phone. Again. s-l-o-w-l-y.

If you've ever felt nervous going into an interview, take heart. And if you've **never** felt nervous going into an interview, take your pulse. It happens to everybody. As I've talked with professionals over the past twenty years, nervousness before a job interview is the same for a million-dollar job ("think about what I have at stake!") as it is for the entry-level gig ("I've never done this before, I'm so nervous.")

So, yes, the job interview is an unusual situation that causes everybody, even me, some anxiety: you're put in a room you've never been, with a person you've never met, to talk about a company you don't work for, to get a job you don't have.

When it finally comes to your interview, we'll split the advice into what the interviewer is trying to accomplish (and what you can do about it), and what you're trying to accomplish (and what you can do about it). In this chapter, I'll take you through 49 questions a thoughtful interviewer in 2020 is likely to ask. We'll also cover what your answers to those questions mean. And I'll share a bag of small tricks that will make interviews seems far less awful.

To start with, why do they want to hire somebody at all? Why has the company decided to interview for this role? What are they hoping to achieve with this new hire?

Why are they hiring?

The economy in 2020 is continuing on its long boom. Unemployment is down, way down. Among college graduates, it's only 2% or so — that's less than half the rate it was at the beginning of the recession.

Demand for employees is up, way up. A couple of years ago, I started asking recruiters and HR departments when they last saw an employment market this strong. For the past few years, it's clearly been the strongest economy we've seen this century. In 2020, it's the strongest any of us have seen in our lifetime.

So the reason you find yourself in an interview room, sitting across from a prospective future boss, is that companies are putting money to work, investing in new projects, and need more people to help them get there. Perhaps your future boss is the visionary who decided to add your possible role, perhaps it was her boss, or her boss's boss. Or maybe the person in the role was lured away by riches promised elsewhere, leaving the role open. In any event, the great economy is the most likely reason behind your interview.

How skilled are companies at interviewing?

With all of this hiring, managers at companies are learning to interview — some for the very first time — and boy, is it an adventure! There are a wide variety of styles for interviewing, and you'll meet interviewers across the entire range, from the pleasant to the flippant to the formal to the casual to the studious to the bizarre. Different companies have different approaches. Different interviewers within the same company have different approaches. The variations in style are as numerous as the traits of human personality.

Sadly, most companies don't have a well-thought-through interview strategy, and it shows. Most hiring managers aren't trained in interviewing, and there are few controls on the dramatic variations. It would be a far better world if there were a few common interview methods that reflected different philosophical approaches to hiring, but the recruitment industry is nowhere near developing even the rudimentary framework to achieve industry standards in this area. There isn't even corporate self-awareness around this problem, and asking HR if there is a consistent company interview style will probably not get you an accurate answer. This leaves you guessing at each individual interviewer's style and doing your best to navigate around the oddities and novelties you encounter. If you do find that there is some consistency between interviewers, consider it a pleasant surprise.

Equally unfortunate, dealing with bad interviewers is par for the course. In the absence of standards, or training, or even coordination, interviewers are left to their own devices. And human beings, given an important task, with little guidance on how to do it, turn to myth, urban legends, and bad advice for their answers. Or even worse, the *internet.*

The hearsay, innuendo, folklore, and personal quirks masquerading as interview strategies can mystify you. Over the years, I've heard numerous hiring managers tell me their favorite interview question, which they trusted as if a guiding star. Whether the candidate had previously worked as a waiter is a common one (always asked by people who had previously been a waiter, as it turns out), whether the candidate can perform well at a series of brainteasers (always asked by people who themselves are good at brain teasers, as it turns out), or whether the candidate liked a particular book, movie, programming language, or ad campaign (always asked by people who liked that particular book, movie, programming language or ad campaign, as it turns out), are frequent crutches.

None of these have anything to do with your ability to do the job for which you're interviewing. There is no research that supports the idea that waiting tables in college, or doing well on brain teasers, or liking a particular book or movie or programming language, give any predictive insight into your future performance in a professional job. Even Google has yielded. Infamous several years ago for its headscratchers, brain teasers, and logical puzzle questions, the company admitted in a New York Times op-ed that many of these practices were useless as interview tools, and had no ability to predict whether or not a professional was going to excel at her job.

Now, if the worst interviewers ask you odd and idiosyncratic questions with little bearing on your performance, the best interviewers are more than happy to let you talk. A truly skilled interviewer finds the topics of most interest to you and steers you toward opening yourself, letting you speak freely on all the subjects you care to address.

And that's dangerous, because a great interviewer can make the conversation feel like it's going much better than it actually is. You'll be chatting away, sharing far more than is judicious, and the whole time your interviewer is patiently writing down the unfiltered evidence both for and against you. You'll get the rope to hang yourself, and, if you're not careful, that's exactly what you'll do.

Answering three things

Your interview is not really about you. Beyond the small talk appropriate to someone at your level, the interviewers aren't tasked with knowing the "real" you, with all your passions, family ties, hobbies, and beliefs. I'll leave the small talk to your discretion, but for professionals in the $100K to $500K range, managing the pleasantries should be a small part of the interview day (an exchange of hellos, a joke about the weather, current hit movie, sports event, or industry gossip, covering three minutes, is about what you should expect).

An interview is not an A&E "Biography Presents", and your interviewer isn't Howard Stern. If you think about it from your future boss's point of view, the interview is not about you, but about how well you fit the needs of his role for which he is hiring. The personal details, your innermost thoughts, your secret interior life… none of them should be in your repertoire for a professional job interview.

The centerpiece of your interview strategy, then, is their three needs. By asking in advance, you've armed yourself with a powerful crystal ball into what topics and questions are likely to be raised in an interview. You'll talk about your ability to do the job, your desire, your motivation, your prior performance and successes, and your career goals, but all within the context of their three needs and how these factors match them.

They might say this position is for a new initiative, or that it is critical for the implementation of an existing strategy, or that the boss needs an expert to help assist in this area. They might share performance targets such as cutting costs by 10 percent, or increasing sales by 15 percent, or cutting website response times by 100 milliseconds. Or they might give you insight into the qualitative improvements, or staff expansion, they're hoping this role will enable.

In *Ladders Resume Guide*, we organized your resume with 25 specific accomplishments, in bullet point form, using a success verb and a specific number or quantification. This is a convenient format for constructing interview answers as well: the success verb underscores your role in taking action, and the quantification shows how you can bring about a positive change, or movement in the right direction. Compare the three most important factors for success in this role to each of your 25 bullet points. Which two or three bullet points and accomplishments on your resume best support your ability to thrive in the role? Which don't speak to any of them? What specific stories or anecdotes about those bullet points can you share to illustrate your capability to do the job?

The best examples showcase your past achievements in an area similar to their three priorities, or demonstrate where your expertise brought about a better outcome. Have you trained staff, performed the work, or led specific projects that demonstrate your ability to achieve each of the three indicated factors? Do you want to highlight your grit, pluck, savvy, polish, determination, cleverness, empathy, persuasiveness, or some other characteristic or capability? Each of your resume bullet points affords you the opportunity to highlight one or more. Picking two or three bullet points for each of the three critical contributors to success, you can string together an effective story of how you can deliver. The more specificity, with greater detail, that you can provide, the more effective your interview will be.

As you review your resume, you also want to consider why your future boss mentioned those three factors, and not others, as her priorities. Do any of the three factors surprise you? Are there follow-up questions you can prepare ahead of time? Do you believe, in your professional opinion, that any of the priorities are misplaced? Or indicative of greater opportunities or deeper challenges? What piques your curiosity about the three priorities and what clarifying questions do you want to explore during the interviews?

By taking the time to review their current needs and your past accomplishments in advance, you will be prepared to discuss each of their three needs in some depth. And that gives you an unfair advantage over the competition, because most candidates come to an interview to talk about themselves and their capabilities, and do relatively little groundwork to find out what the hiring manager of the company believes she needs.

Speaking of which, how do you feel your competition for this role will fare on the three key factors? Is the number of people with those attributes or capabilities pretty large, or is the pool fairly small? Are there areas where others will outshine you? Or where you are stronger than the typical person in your field? How do your guesses about the competition change your strategy about how you discuss the three requirements, or the stories that you'll use to illustrate them? Should you emphasize a particular specialty that you are dominant in, or stick with a broader coverage of all three? Each scenario or possibility merits some thought, and there's no right answer. However, spending the time to think about your competition will make you better prepared to address issues and ask questions.

The better you think through all of your material, the more prepared you will be to stay "on message." You may have noticed that people being interviewed on TV rarely say "I have no answer for that" and always seem to come up with something charming, witty, or polished to offer in response to the question. They're out promoting their new book, or movie, or show, and they always bring the conversation back around to that new venture. If you happen to catch them on more than one show, perhaps you've been surprised that the star will be more consistent in telling their same story the same way twice than you are in recounting what you had for breakfast. Lady Gaga even found herself gently mocked at the 2019 Grammys for her precisely repeated praise of co-star Bradley Cooper: "There can be 100 people in a room and 99 of those people won't believe in you, but you just need one to believe in you."

A lot of it is show biz, sure, and it's what they do for a living, but it also involves a lot of careful preparation. Appearing that graceful and well-studied doesn't come by accident, it comes by practice. The PR folks and the agents and the advisors all flutter around the star for weeks beforehand, making sure that the message they're sharing about the film or the show or the book is consistent, helpful, and to the point, 99 times out of 100.

You, in the meantime, are the star of your own movie. And for each interview or set of interviews with a company, you will have your own remarkably consistent answers, based on their three most important needs. By crafting interview answers in advance that speak to what is most interesting and important to **your** audience, you'll come across just as practiced and polished as those Hollywood movie stars, and stand out from other candidates. By the way, this forms the basis for my advice that professionals should not try to craft **different** resumes for each company, rather, they should craft different stories for each company from the **same** resume document.

It makes sense to reconfirm with each interviewer what they view as the three most important factors for success in the job. You might repeat what you heard from HR and ask if that matches up with their viewpoint. Should the differences among multiple interviewers be **too** different, you may raise the issue with your future boss for clarification — it's difficult to succeed in a role when your colleagues don't agree on "what success looks like."

Using their three success factors as a recurring theme in your answers not only makes you look responsive to their needs, but is a very effective way to structure your interview time. If you have three examples for each of the three factors, and you have practiced enough to spend five minutes on each, you're well prepared to manage any amount of discussion up to 45 minutes without breaking a sweat. You'll never be at a loss for words, because you can always continue the interview by asking if they'd like to hear *another* way you can help them hit one of the three goals.

Because interviewers are generally not well-trained, their conversation may veer off into college sports, or the latest restaurant opening, or, heaven forbid, politics. When any of these happen, steer the talk back to how you can contribute on the three key needs — you will always have a reliable way to tell your story in a positive, relevant, light. Stay "on message" and when you walk out, your message will stay behind with your future boss.

Behavioral interviewing

Interestingly, this connection between past performance and future success underpins the biggest change over the past decade in how companies interview and select employees.

Companies have discovered that social interviews are ineffective. Social interviews are unstructured conversations that are allowed to flow wherever the participants allow them to, usually toward some shared social group, activity, or bonding. The worst of this kind of interview is the type depicted in *Mad Men*, where two middle-aged boozehounds chat over bourbons and swap war stories until they both end up poured into taxicabs at the end of the evening. This interview style, which focused on sociability and a certain type of agreeableness, has proven to be a very poor predictor of success or future performance in a job.

Replacing boozy nights and Googly brain teasers, the behavioral interview hopes to assess the future performance of a candidate by understanding, in detail, what the candidate has done in the past.

Behavioral interviews are structured around asking about past behavior in specific situations, the candidate's responses to past challenges, and emotional and behavioral reactions to past conflicts, so that the interviewer can create a picture of how the candidate typically performs in various scenarios. Someone who enjoyed inspiring a sales team to beat quota, hated working alone on spreadsheets, and preferred the comfort of cold, hard cash to flighty theories about potential future revenues, is most likely to do so again in the future. And the reverse holds true — people who didn't like doing those things will tend to not like them in the future either.

Behavioral interview questions tend toward a structure similar to "Tell me about a time when…" or "Describe for me a time when …" or sometimes the indirect route, "What would your boss / coworkers / team members / assistant say about your…" These questions are structured to elicit specific information about your past experiences, your reactions to them, your course of action, your outcomes, and your reflections.

The academic research supporting behavioral interviewing underscores the uselessness of social interviews, interviews about hypothetical future scenarios, or brain teaser interviews. The anecdotal feedback on behavioral interviews is favorable, too. Behavioral interviews appear to help companies hire better, understand candidates more thoroughly, and make a better match between person and role. As a result, it has become the dominant interviewing style favored by giants as varied as Google and GE.

Perhaps the best, and most obvious reminder, is that in a world where past performance matters, the best way to interview well is to perform well. Outstanding performance, year after year, in a variety of positions, situations, and contexts, builds the most confidence among interviewers in your ability to perform well in the future.

As a result, it will be useful for you to review 49 specific behavioral questions. The variety of behavioral questions are innumerable, and the various formats they take would fill… a Kindle, I guess. We won't have time to list all of them, or even a substantial portion, if we want to get through this Interviews Guide in 90 minutes. So I've picked seven subject matter areas and shared seven specific questions in each, sometimes as multi-part questions.

Following each section of questions, I share with you the answers interviewers expect from great performers, the answers they're disappointed to get from bad performers, and, where relevant, the answers they get from people who simply have no experience in the subject matter.

I've picked questions from a variety of sources commonly used by HR managers and recruiters, including the granddaddy of them all, *Topgrading* **by Bradford D. Smart, Ph.D**. These questions are broadly applicable to a wide range of professionals: leading individual contributors, managers, middle managers, and upper management executives. You should answer at the level appropriate to your experience and expertise. I've grouped the questions into seven relevant categories. With that, let's review the topics, questions, and good and bad answers to our behavioral questions below:

Teamwork

1. When I speak with your current boss or coworkers, how much of a team player will they say you are?

2. How have your teams gotten better? What did you do to improve team skills, cohesion, performance, or output?

3. Describe for me the best hire you've ever made. And how about the worst? Which have been your best-performing and most disappointing teams in your recent roles?

4. What have been the biggest challenges to teamwork you've faced in your recent role? What was your approach to improving that teamwork?

5. What's the worst fight you've managed between two subordinates in your recent role? How did you have them resolve their conflict?

6. How have you presented your work to coworkers or people outside of your area of specialty?

7. Tell me about a time you worked with someone you personally disliked. What was your approach to communicate your displeasure with them? With managing the work with them? How did they perform on the tasks? How about your experience working with someone who was difficult to work with, or personally irritating to you? Can you describe for me a time that happened?

Great performers reveal their commitment to team success and team goals. They are able to point out specific instances where their coworkers led or helped the team to great achievements. They attribute the successes of their teams to the actions and initiative of their team members or colleagues. They praise their peers for their positive attributes and can explain how each of the weaknesses on the team was matched by a strength, or was handled by teams agreeing to share the load.

Great performers actively work to manage through discord or conflict on their teams. If they're able to find a way to mitigate negative feelings or behaviors, they do, and if they can't, they assist team members in coping to the best of their ability. They enlist the aid of their boss or superior in monitoring and improving team dynamics, and provide thoughtful input on courses of action without "speaking out of school."

They work through personality differences or difficulties with a professional demeanor, and try to focus their teams on the output expected of them. At their best, they push for a team to achieve its potential from a position of peer leadership.

Great performers seek ways to make their team even better through social and professional bonding. They participate in or encourage casual interactions outside the formal environment of work. And they encourage or enable their colleagues to improve their professional abilities through conferences, classes, or training.

Bad performers find ways to assign their lack of success to their teammates. They are quick to find fault with the foibles of others, and can easily recite a lengthy list of letdowns from their peers. They catalog the failings of their colleagues in some detail, and, at their worst, show some perverse enjoyment in the telling of sad stories. While they are able to recount conflict in great detail, they did little to fix it, and in some cases, perhaps encouraged it.

When it comes to team dynamics, they are "nobody's fool," and "won't take that kind of thing lying down." They "fight for what is rightfully theirs," because "you gotta get your piece of the pie" even at the expense of coworkers. It's what smart people do, according to bad performers.

They actively throw their former bosses and coworkers under the bus, and lay blame for shortcomings at their feet. Even small bumps or hurdles in working with others were sufficient to prevent bad performers from achieving their daily, weekly, monthly, or annual goals. Fresh new obstacles were strewn in their path with some regularity by their ungrateful peers.

Bad performers have unproductive negative emotions that cripple their ability to achieve professionally. They either do not participate in the growth of the team, or actively undermine it through envy, self-absorption, or incompetence.

Non-performers have been individual contributors or opted out of team-related work. They have primarily focused on improving their own skills and abilities and have had little desire or need to contribute to a team. With little past experience, they should spend time reflecting on their desire to be in a team, and why that might or might not work out well.

*(After each section, please review your resume, and determine which bullet points and which stories you might address to each of the seven questions, and how you might be able to cast your experience in a light similar to that of the great performers. All of us being human, you should also review your stories in relation to what bad performers do and say, and reflect on when you have not performed your best. Situations where you unfortunately modeled the behavior of bad performers can be blind spots, and if you blurt out negative or counter-productive answers during an interview, it can be fatal to your larger story. **Before** the interview is a better time to reflect, reconsider, and repent.)*

Performance

1. Tell me about a time you introduced efficiency improvements in your current role.
2. What has been your most successful job in your career? The least successful?

3. What work or accomplishment are you most proud of? What was your role in the achievement? Why is this your most proud accomplishment?

4. How did you improve top-line growth at your prior role? Tell me about a time your advice to your boss resulted in increased revenues? Lower costs? Greater profitability?

5. What's been your most important contribution to your current team or company? Whose idea was it? How did it come about and get approved and implemented?

6. How did you improve expense management, or reduce costs, at your prior role?

7. What are the biggest risks you've taken in your most recent role? How did they work out?

Great performers set goals and achieve them. They are able to bring the resources, planning, and willpower to bear on an area of importance to their company and deliver the results. Even if their day-to-day work is far removed from bringing in revenue or reducing costs, they are able to connect the dots between their efforts and the company's top-line financial goals and results.

They take stretch assignments that don't always work out well, but reflect positively upon themselves as ambitious go-getters. Whether or not their riskier assignments delivered improved financial results, they learned good lessons from the experience and were able to keep a positive attitude about their work, team, and company.

They are proud of work that made a meaningful difference for the company, even when the personal glory was not proportionate. Projects that call on multiple aptitudes and capabilities make great performers happy because success requires managing many collaborators: bosses, peers, subordinates, partners — and diverse resources: materials, tools, research, content, physical goods.

They consistently seek to improve their company and team quantitatively. Because of their team's performance the company was measurably better, by percentages, by dollars, or by degree.

Great performers understand what their company or boss needs and are able to conceptualize new solutions that address problems or needs effectively. They are able to implement those plans and create a better outcome for their team or company.

Bad performers have been unable to deliver results for a variety of wide-ranging reasons. Their boss or superiors were unsupportive of their goals, or changed their minds frequently. Their peers had conflicting desires or political agendas that did not line up with their own. Their subordinates were under-paid, under-qualified, poorly-trained, or incompetent. The resources they were allotted were insufficient to the task, poorly assigned, or deficient in quality, quantity or type. They did the best they could with what they were given, even if the outcome wasn't close to the goals.

Reasons for failures often focus on what was best for the bad performer as an individual rather than the company's needs. It is difficult for poor performers to be at their best when so many around them are not assisting or delivering in the right way.

Bad performers don't like the spotlight of accountability and seek to avoid it if at all possible. Measurements and quantification are inappropriate for their area because others don't understand the qualitative importance of what the bad performer does — those who think that way are philistines or worse, in the eyes of the bad performer. They prefer to check the boxes when requested and implement the routine work assigned to them by others.

Non performers have not yet been called upon to be excellent. They have studied, or consulted, or carried out the plans of others and have only been required to comply with orders or requests given. They've not shown an ability to engage in multi-day or multi-month planning. Non-performers should consider whether they will enjoy being responsible for outcomes and judged on performance, or prefer a less demanding, more directed role.

Intelligence & capacity for learning

1. Tell me about a time you had to consume a large amount of data and assess what was important and what was not.

2. What will peers say about your ability to dig into facts beyond what is expected of you? Can you provide an example?

3. Do you prefer to deal in facts or concepts? The reality of the present, or the possibility of the future? Do you dig into the details, or are you more interested in the bigger picture?

4. Tell me about a time you were very creative in your most recent role.

5. Describe a complicated situation in which you had to learn a lot quickly. What was your approach?

6. How do you stay up-to-date with the latest trends, software, and management practices in our industry? What trends have you decided to not spend time following? What are the most overrated and most underrated trends? What are your reading, viewing, conference-going habits? What's most effective for your professional development and why?

7. What's your biggest disagreement with the conventional wisdom about where the industry is going?

Great performers exhibit a curiosity about the world, their business and their customers that is natural, authentic, and engaging. They like to make predictions about where things will head and compare them to what really happens in order to obtain a better understanding of the world. They are consistently setting new targets or new goals for learning.

They have a great capacity and appetite for picking up new fields of interest. They have routinized a methodology to learn new things — whether it's by reading, attending seminars, watching videos, or learning-by-doing. They understand what they learn well and how they learn well.

Great performers drill down to the root cause. They see beyond the surface level symptoms to grasp at the underlying causes. They have experienced the thrill of new skills and new talents, and the challenge of taking on new areas without much prior understanding. They like the feeling of being slightly off-kilter in a new domain and pushing themselves to master new material as efficiently as possible.

They are adept at utilizing experts, peers, or advisors to get insight into where and how they should learn, so as to best direct their own learning time. They have acquired the educated person's capability to listen respectfully to experts, and then make their own assessments. As a result, they have a shrewd sense of where the crowd is right or wrong and a healthy skepticism that they have landed on the correct answer for all times and all situations.

Bad performers are pleased with their current level of knowledge. It took a lot of effort to get here, and now that they are here, they're going to enjoy the fruits of those efforts. Additional effort at learning is misplaced, as the payoff for learning new things or developing new skills is, honestly, to be assigned more work. Bad performers view lifelong learners as suck-ups and show-offs, and don't need to associate with their kind.

They try to focus on the known facts, and will apply an existing model to the problem, as that is likely to take the least time. Old ways are tried and true, and even if the situation might have been better off with a review of the current needs, it's unlikely anybody is going to get in trouble sticking with the existing solution. When the boss or team needs something new done, the best response is to make sure to acquire the outside resource or expert who can answer the question for them.

Performance Management

1. How many performance reviews have you completed with your team in the past year? What's your process for performance management and reviews? What has improved as a result?

2. What would your coworkers say is your approach to managing out underperformers? When a team member is underperforming, what has been your approach for letting them know? Do you take responsibility? How did you motivate them?

3. Tell me about a time you managed an employee who disregarded your requests. How did you manage the situation?

4. Are you a hands-off or hands-on manager? How effective are your methods for delegating, following up, and assessing performance on assignments made to your team?

5. How do you manage your compensation review process? Who gets raises from you and why? Is it equal across the board each year, or do you vary by performance?

6. Tell me about a time a manager, colleague or team member came to you with a problem they couldn't solve, what did you do?

7. Walk me through your most recent team. Person by person, who were the A's, B's, and C's? How were A's rewarded? How were B's improved? How were C's managed out?

Great performers have a means or methodology for eliciting the best performance from their teams and reports. They match their management style to the needs of the team member rather than taking a one-size-fits-all approach. They provide an appropriate level and style of guidance and feedback to their team members, and monitor the impact of their methods on their team members' output. They schedule, and honor, regular 1-on-1s with their subordinates and superiors.

Great performers are able to identify, in collaboration with each team member, areas for growth, and strengths that should be developed. They structure the work, training and development time for each team member to improve their performance, skills, and capabilities over time.

They set reasonable or sensible targets with their team members, and monitor performance appropriately for the level of work. They have a method for delegating work, or not delegating work in order to keep a closer watch on team members requiring supervision.

They pay top performers more than low performers, and have the courage to share their assessments with each annually. When problems arise with a team member's performance, they have an effective means for managing the size of the problem down. They take steps to address and improve performance. And when change in behavior and performance is not forthcoming, they exit under-performers humanely.

Bad performers view performance management as outside their purview. Their team members have been hired to do a job, so they are probably doing it. They don't want to take away from their own job in order to review and bother with the output of the professionals on their team. They expect that things will work out fine.

They see their team members every day, or frequently enough, and talk to them informally and casually all the time, so there's no need to create a formal or 1-on-1 meeting structure. Annual reviews don't change much about people's outcomes or behaviors, so they're a waste of time as well.

The company or team will produce about the amount of results it is going to produce, and as long as the bad performer follows the rules and checks the boxes, they can't really be blamed for how things turn out.

Non performers in this area have not managed a team yet, or have purposely stayed in an individual contributor role. Non-performers should consider how the new field of people management — which is likely far different than their field of expertise — varies from their past behaviors and successes, and whether taking on this new kind of challenge will be intrinsically rewarding to them.

Management Work

1. Describe how you like to run meetings. Have you changed how you've run meetings in recent years?

2. Tell me about a time you trimmed the amount of work in a project in order to match what the team could actually accomplish. How did you secure permission, communicate the decision, manage the process, and what was the outcome with your boss?

3. What has been your approach to training new team members? What would you change about how prior employers have managed training? How do you approach training and development of team members?

4. How do you report progress to your manager? When have you reached out for help? When do you decide not to bother them? What's your approach to "managing up"?

5. What are the most difficult changes you've had to manage in your organization or team in recent years?

6. What do you believe is important for a healthy work environment? How have you helped create that environment at your current role?

7. How do you like to structure your 1-on-1s? How are agendas set, schedules made, follow up assigned? What would you improve?

Great performers have a basket of tools and tricks that have developed over time to help them accomplish the work at hand. No one tool is right for every purpose or need, so great performers experiment over time and seek to learn from others what works best to achieve desired outcomes. They enjoy the craft of management and seek to practice it. They have a reasonable sense of humor and humility about their own capability to manage, and greet setbacks and challenges with a positive outlook and determination without letting themselves get too down.

They are respectful of their team members' and coworkers' time and try to match the need for meetings to necessary outcomes. When work, deadlines, or projects are scheduled too tightly, or too loosely, they rally support to adjust accordingly.

They've learned the ins and outs of different approaches to management, and how those approaches work with different personalities, situations, timeframes, and environments. They also know which ones they prefer, and loathe, and manage their own emotional reactions to practices that are required for success, even if unenjoyable for themselves.

They manage on a 360-degree basis, understanding that their reports, peers, and bosses have different needs and desired outcomes from their interactions. They also have a means for onboarding new team members, bringing them into the fold, and enabling their professional development. They seek help when needed, but otherwise try to be self-sufficient.

Bad performers know that meetings are part of office life, and there's not much you can do to change it. At least they can multitask with their phone under the table while others are blathering on.

Bad performers know that if they have enough projects with enough conflicting deadlines, they can always avoid having any one of them be singled out for non-performance. In the long run, they'll all get done, so it doesn't make too much sense to create stress about any particular one.

Nobody really enjoys work, but it's a kind of necessary evil, so it's best to find ways to compensate yourself for the pain. Offsites for skiing, near beaches, or in cool cities, are great team bonding exercises that are also easy on the personal pocketbook.

Managers are always asking for some kind of numbers, and the most effective way to handle these requests is to hand them over to your reports. After all, the ambitious up-and-comer wants my job, so why shouldn't I let him do it? There's always a need for more information it seems, but if you can send enough information in a dense enough packet up to your bosses, they'll never have time to review it all.

Bad performers know to never show weakness, as that leads to setbacks or uncomfortable questions. At the same time, who is to blame them if they help their rivals fail a little bit by making sure the bosses know when they goof things up?

Leadership

1. When have people followed your lead? When have they not? Are you usually the leader of a team or group in the office? Why do you think people follow you?
2. Describe for me a policy you don't agree with at your current role. How did you ensure compliance?
3. Tell me about a time you made or enforced an unpopular decision.
4. How do you hire? What's your process for recruiting, interviewing, selecting, offering, and closing new team members? Tell me about the hiring process in your current or prior role? What worked well, and what would you change? What's your approach to hiring in a competitive market? How have you landed talent needed to fill your team?
5. What motivates your team? How do you motivate a team when it becomes disengaged, discouraged, or demoralized? How do you *keep* your teams motivated? What sets your team back the most: tight deadlines, high performance standards, cost constraints, or something else?

6. Describe a time you were asked to lead a cross-team project. How did you manage task assignment, follow-up and completion? What tools did you use to keep the project on time?

7. Tell me about a time you had to develop and implement a new policy. What steps did you take? What did not go well? How did you handle that?

Great performers take a personal role in leading team members, peers, and other employees to success and are able to inspire outstanding performance through a variety of personal, situational, and instructional leadership. Great leaders shoulder blame, share credit, and take responsibility. They understand that leadership is sometimes about being unpopular and are willing to suffer this personal pain for the greater good of the team or company.

Great performers know that great recruiting is essential to their success, and spend a disproportionate amount of time focused on it. They seek to recruit, attract, and retain the best players in each of the roles on their team, and push their organization to do what's necessary to achieve this lofty goal.

Great performers lead with an understanding that leadership often requires others to change their behavior in some way — change tasks, or time, or communication, or method, or environment — and that change is usually unpopular. Great performers put in the time and effort and communications systems to overcome this common human resistance to change.

Great performers are very good communicators and seek to communicate early, often and everywhere. They understand that repetition of messaging is most effective at making sure they are heard and aren't afraid to communicate a message repeatedly.

Bad performers know it's not their fault.

Companies are always implementing stupid policies and it's best to make sure that the team knows you're on their side, and that you think the higher ups are fools, too.

Being unpopular for the sake of a company is a bad idea, it creates too much stress in the day-to-day work, and doesn't really change anything anyway. Bad performers seek to evade being the bearer of bad news, the face of unpopular policies, or the disciplinarian on expenses.

Hiring is difficult. We don't have enough money, resources, team members, or cool projects to work on here, so it's pretty understandable that we're not going to get the rock stars. B players are all we can get, so we had better get used to it.

Bad performers are just passing along the tasks. They can't help it if the tasks sent down from above don't make sense, or aren't what we were doing yesterday. After all, what are you going to do?

Bad performers don't spend much time or effort thinking about team morale or motivation, but when they do, they know who's to blame — management. They have ideas about how management could improve morale around here, but don't push too hard to get themselves heard because it's not their job anyway. But they could definitely do a better job than their bosses if they wanted to.

Non performers are low-level managers or individual contributors who have not yet been called on to show leadership beyond their immediate tasks. They are accustomed to being judged on the specific tasks that have been assigned to them. In contemplating opportunities higher up in the hierarchy, they should consider whether or not they'd enjoy being held accountable for outcomes, both tangible and intangible, rather than just task completion.

Organizational

1. What's been your role in your company's most recent organizational changes? How have you managed and communicated those changes to your team?
2. Are your peers political? How have you managed office politics?

3. Tell me about a project you were on, led, or conceived that subsequently failed. What went wrong and why? How did you recover?

4. How have you helped or advised your company to handle internet-related dangers — data breaches, internet security, fake news — in 2020? What are your thoughts on best practices to ensure team compliance with security policies?

5. How have you helped set realistic deadlines? How do you manage unrealistic deadlines imposed on you?

6. What was your role in last year's budget? What was the outcome? What were you happy or unhappy with?

7. How have you ensured your team's goals are aligned with the company's?

Great performers have an ability to navigate organizations to achieve goals. All companies are political, but great performers seek to minimize the impact of politics, build bridges with other teams, and actively tear down walls to constructive teamwork, in order to achieve organizational objectives.

They are effective at communicating the company's goals and needs to their team and peers. They are also effective at knowing when not to filter the bad news and communicate unusual dissatisfaction or front-line facts upwards.

They model and celebrate the behaviors essential to the company's success. Knowing that you don't get the behavior you deserve, you get the behavior you reward, they seek to reward the desired behaviors on their teams.

They understand how to foster conflict in a positive way that contributes to the company's success.

They have a concern for the company's health over and above their team's health and outcomes, or personal considerations. They seek to be good citizens and always act in the best interests of the company, regardless of whether or not someone is watching. They're mindful of the future and don't shortchange tomorrow to pay for today.

They will make sacrifices of time, career, or preference if the company requires it, to a reasonable degree. They'll take appropriate risks for the benefit or furtherance of the company's interests.

Bad performers are ineffective in their organizations, usually due to the incompetence of others. They understand that politics are the way the game is played, and they are not going to be blindsided or tie their own hands behind their back when there are so many devious people in the company.

They focus on their own outcomes, and don't need to be concerned with the company's outcomes. It's a corporation after all, and it can take care of itself.

They are oblivious or indifferent to the impact their behavior has on their teams and peers, and seek to optimize their own comfort and rewards, even if at the expense of others.

(Again, please match bullet points and stories to address to each of the seven questions across each of the seven sections. This detailed matching of stories on your resume to questions in an interview make for the most compelling and effective answers.)

At the time of publication, we had an additional 10 behavioral question sets on our companion web page at **https://www.theladders.com/career-advice/interviews-guide**, and we'll keep adding to the list.

Specialty interviews

Along the way, you may be called upon to do the remote interview or phone screen. Keeping a good attitude and upbeat presence on these calls is as important as having great answers. Toward that end, **buy a mirror or have your phone camera available to do an interview selfie**. Under pressure, and perhaps trying to maintain good confidentiality, professionals tend to hunch during interview phone calls, which gives them bad posture, poor breathing, and an ineffective vocal presence.

Use the mirror or your phone camera to watch your expression. When you look at your own face, you tend to smile more and frown less. And smiling, according to a growing body of research, in and of itself tends to bring on a better mood and a higher energy level. And that will come across in a better, more positive tone of voice on the phone.

Also on phone and video interviews, make sure to clear the background of visual or sound clutter. Odd potted plants, a too colorful Jimi Hendrix print, or a direct view into your walk-in closet, can prove distracting. Mindful of the example of the BBC expert whose 4-year-old pranced in the back of his video frame on TV, please clear the children in addition to the clutter. It also makes sense to call in five minutes ahead of time, to avoid mishaps.

You may also be called upon to do a specialized interview such as the consultant case interview, the coding interview, the screen test, or the live demo sales test, which are frequent enough that you should master the particular ones in your field. These specialist, or role-specific, interviews seek to understand your mastery of the body of knowledge relevant to that area and how you use your judgment in applying that understanding to real world problems.

These specialist interviews are outside the scope of this 90-minute book, so I've not included role-specific questions or interview practices, and have instead focused on addressing interview themes common to all professionals. There are a wide variety of offline and online specialty materials that address the more detailed needs of role-specific interviews, and I encourage you to seek them out to complement the more general advice in this guide.

#Interviewfails

We all have pet peeves, blind spots, and character flaws. Occasionally they sneak into your interviews…

Coming out of business school, I'd scored a great interview opportunity with a top investment firm in New York. I'd had a few great rounds with the team, and on this particular day, I was meeting with a "name" partner — one of the big guns who had founded the firm and whose name was on the door.

This senior partner was the kind of imperious fellow who'd later be photographed in Bermuda shorts riding ponies on his Carribean estate in the Wall Street Journal Weekend Edition. Frankly speaking, not my cup of tea. So when he dropped my least favorite interview question of all time — the question that forever marks you as a careless, sloppy nitwit because it is so meaningless and begs for such phoniness — I snapped.

Yes, it was that awful old #interviewfail: "What's your greatest weakness?"

So I guess my impishness got the better of me, and I looked him straight in the eye and replied: "Brevity."

And not saying another word, stared politely right back at him. Probably with a little bit of a wise-ass grin, as the seconds stretched along into a nice quiet awkward impasse. It was pretty juvenile, and I'd let my joker get the better of me. Things went downhill from there, and the interview ended with a polite "don't-let-the-door-hit-you-on-the-way-out" pat on the back a few minutes later.

I'd blown the interview and felt like schmuck. OK, maybe 50 percent schmuck and 50 percent vindicated avenger of suffering interviewees everywhere. But in any event, it was a great opportunity and I'd killed it with a smarmy, smart aleck reply.

Something similar — a goof, a slip, a personality quirk — has happened to you before and will happen to you again. At some points in your career, you'll really botch an interview. Like everything worthwhile in life, you'll just need to dust yourself off and try again — it's how you handle the recovery that marks your professionalism. In the best cases, you'll at least have a funny story to share years later in a book you write about interviews.

There are also unfortunate questions — illegal, unethical, or immoral questions that interviewers ask candidates because it popped into their head, or because they want to know, regardless of the rule of law. Most interviewers aren't trained, so if you feel aggrieved, remember that they feel uncertain. While we wish that all interviewers approached their duties with the seriousness of purpose with which you approach yours, that's generally an unfulfilled dream.

If you get callow, but nonetheless illegal, questions about race, pregnancy, disability, or any other aspect of your life about which you should not be getting questions, you'll need to decide how to handle it. You may perhaps decide to have a bit of sympathy (once) and then move the conversation back to the relevant stuff. At a later time or date, you can reflect on the experience and make a reasoned decision about whether you'd like to continue to engage with an employer, future colleague, or boss, with such a haphazard approach to weighty topics. Blatant, purposeful, or explicit discrimination in these areas can not and should not be explained away — don't talk yourself into believing it will get better, because it won't. If this is how the firm behaves when it is trying to impress, things will be much worse day to day. It is best to turn tail and make for the exit as quickly as possible.

In 2020, it's increasingly illegal to ask your current compensation. This has always been an irrelevant question, and I've long counseled professionals to demur politely when asked. After all, you're negotiating the appropriate price for future work, not rehashing whether or not your past work was adequately compensated. Focus the conversation on your target compensation or the pay level offered by the interviewing firm. This provides you with an opportunity to improve your pay, especially if your prior employer had a monetary setback or reduced wages for or non-performance-related reasons.

I mentioned earlier that some interviewers cling to weird superstitions and fixate on a pet question to which they ascribe inordinate powers of prediction. "This is my lucky question" is the kind of magical thinking that does not belong in a modern interview, but nonetheless, there it is. If you can, dissuade your interviewer with a polite redirection. "What are the best answers you get?" is a good way to not answer the question and move the conversation along.

And from their point of view, what **don't** interviewers want to hear? What are #interviewfails you should avoid?

They don't want to hear you trash-talk your former or current employer. On the principle of "bad-mouth thee, bad-mouth me," your interviewer — legitimately — worries that if you're willing to throw your present employer under the bus in a conversation with strangers, your interviewer, too, will face the same fate at some point in the future. Never, ever, say a bad, mean or unkind thing — *especially* if it's true — because that displays your ability to be an ingrate, a gossip, and a ne'er-do-well.

They don't want to hear arrogance or timidity. An overburdened sense of self, or an underdeveloped self-confidence are both worrying to employers in the heavily collaborative workplace of 2020.

They also prefer to not be on the receiving end of wandering, meandering, drifting answers. If they're wondering when your answer is going to end, you've gone on too long. If you've had problems with long-windedness in the past, practice until you get yourself out of the habit. Your iPhone or Android have convenient timers and voice memo recording. Use some of your practice hours to record yourself giving two minute answers to the questions above. If you can't bring the answer in under 120 seconds, then start over and do it again, and again, until you can.

Interviewers definitely do not want to be a forum for your alternative career development plans. You may be tempted to dwell on issues such as how difficult the job search is (ok, yes it is, so how is talking about it going to help shorten your job search?), or what your perfect career would be (we're not here to talk about your perfect career, we're here to talk about this job and who we should hire for it). You should resist the temptation.

Interviewers do not want to hear your company's confidential information. Well, ethical interviewers anyway. With the precedent of Uber coughing up $250 million for their Google recruit's ethical lapses in mishandling trade secrets, no company should want to hear your employer's secrets. And I'm sure my readers share an ethical backbone that would prevent them from ever considering such a course of action in the first place.

Interviewers prefer not to hear all of your answers in corporate voice — you know, the tone and vocabulary of an annual report, rather than a backyard BBQ. You should instead try to sound like the worker or coworker you are going to be — approachable, human, normal. A level of formality that falls between your college reunion and your spouse's work event is probably in the right range.

At its essence, interviewers don't want to see in an interview the behaviors they don't want to see in the workplace. If interviews are predictions of the career ahead, you want to be a positive, capable, effective person they'll look forward to spending their workdays with.

And finally, you may ask, if so many interviewers are untrained, how likely is it that I'll be on the receiving end of a behavioral interview, anyway? Won't the interviewers just be winging it the way they've always done? The answer is, in part, yes.

While interviewers are by and large not trained, the behavioral interview advice and training they are ignoring is nonetheless influential. It seeps into the process through example questions, discussions of answers from people who do interview behaviorally, and expectations communicated from HR. Further, the HR person or recruiter is far more likely to have undergone training for behavioral interviewing and is more likely to ask you questions similar in tenor and tone to those above.

In any event, behavioral questions being more substantial and piercing than prior generations of interview questions, if you train yourself to master these, you'll be able to handle any others with style.

4. DURING THE INTERVIEW: 25 QUESTIONS YOU'LL ASK THEM

If someone asked you to invest a half-million bucks into a business plan, how much time would you spend reviewing the details of that business plan, meeting the people behind it and doing your research? What if the amount you were investing was $1 million? Or $2 million? Given your present net worth, how long and how carefully would you consider that investment? I'm guessing your answer would be that you'd investigate pretty thoroughly as those are large sums of money.

Have you considered that your next job is exactly such a large investment? You're trading the next four or five years of your life — you are *investing* the next four or five years of your life — in exchange for the work experience and the cash you'll get paid. For the typical Ladders member that's a half-million dollars or more.

The amount of time to invest in carefully considering your next career investment *should* be days or weeks or months. Your human capital — your time and effort over the years to come — is your most significant investment. Not only does it likely represent the vast majority of your earnings, it also has a disproportionate impact on your mental health, your mood, your satisfaction, your contentment.

I have observed many professionals get "caught up in the moment" and make life-altering decisions essentially on a whim, or without sufficient forethought. Some spend more time studying the car they purchase than the job they take, even though an automobile represents 1/10th or 1/20th the size of investment they're making in their new employer. The compelling nature of the interview process, the friendly faces and kind words with which you'll be greeted, the glittering promises and future bonanza they'll promise you, all work to sweep even sober-minded professionals off their feet.

Ensuring that a role is a good fit for you is as essential to good interviewing as answering their questions. Sharing with your interviewer that "I'd like to figure out if this role is right for me," is productive, forthright and fresh. It's also disarming and direct. It shows that you have the self-possession to understand that not only do you need to display the ability to do the job, but also that you have standards and criteria against which you'll measure this opportunity.

Back in Section 2, I asked you to write down three to four company-specific questions for you to use in the interview. Now is the time to deploy them. Asking a few questions that refer specifically to the operations of the company is helpful to you on three levels.

First, you can compare answers across interviewers, and see how different people from the company answer the same high-level questions. Second, it shows that you're the type of person who is prepared for the tasks you undertake, and that you approach significant decisions seriously. Third, it signals a strong interest in the company, as, believe it or not, most interviewees don't show up with much in the way of questions or research at all.

Please note that context matters with these questions. Asking why Q3 margins in China were so low is overweening for a regional marketing manager at an Atlanta Chick-Fil-A interviewing for a job at KFC, but exactly expected for someone interviewing for the top job in logistics at Apple. Don't get too cute or too clever.

Active listening

Your best method for determining if a position matches with your needs is to ask revealing questions that allow you to understand the company, its culture, and its operations much better than "so tell me what it's like to work here." I've assembled 25 questions that will give you a terrific level of insight into any company at which you interview.

To be slightly tongue-in-cheek, the rule for job interviews is: "He who talks the least, wins." If you can get your interviewer talking about their viewpoints, their job, and their hopes for this new role, you'll be collecting a lot more information about what it takes to get the job. You can make your own points effectively in as little as 10 minutes, and have plenty of time to allow your interviewers to speak expansively about their own thoughts.

The goal of asking questions is to **listen**. As the greatest salespeople will tell you, listening is the most important skill in any conversation. You want to listen to what people tell you, because that is how you'll get a more accurate picture of what is really wanted, and whether or not you will be successful there.

It's also a truism that the more your interviewer speaks, the smarter you are. If you can ask good, open-ended questions that get the interviewer talking about her current role, you tend to get assigned much greater marks for intellectual capability and business wisdom.

Active listening means being a good conversationalist — reacting appropriately, asking follow-up questions, frowning at the sad parts, smiling at the successes — that your interviewer shares with you. It also means demonstrating that you're processing what they're saying, not merely nodding in their direction. There are generic active listening questions you can always rely on — past / present / future questions of the type: "What would you have done differently in the past?" "Are you pleased with the way it's turned out?", and "What would need to change in the future for the outcome to be different?" You can generate a lot of mileage out of past / present / future questions, and most executives love answering them.

What commonly gets in the way of listening is your own voice. You may talk about yourself for too long, and share a level of detail out of proportion to the question asked. Or your nerves get a hold of you and you find yourself with a case of motormouth, filling up the air space with talk to reduce the tension you feel inside. With more practice, either in private or in real world interviews, this improves if you focus on delivering concise answers and eliciting long responses.

In addition to gathering general intelligence on the role and opportunity, you're also listening for **roadblocks** or **opt-outs**.

Roadblocks are the decisions they've made about the role and who they're looking for that don't match up with your background, experience, skills or talents. Determine as quickly as possible if those roadblocks mean there is little chance for your successful candidacy for the position. For example, are they looking for people from a different industry, different experience level, different background from yours?

When it comes to roadblocks, you may be tempted to use strong arguments to talk them out of their viewpoint. But this response rarely works. Because roadblocks have been agreed to by the interview group, it is highly unlikely that an outsider is going to persuade that group to change its mind. When they've made a reasoned decision to hire a different array of skills and experience for the role, it's pointless to try and change their decision in your favor. You generally won't have the face-time, the credibility, or the institutional knowledge to make a persuasive case. In these situations, politely bow out of the running and focus your time on more productive opportunities.

Opt-outs are features of the job or characteristics of the opportunity that don't match up with your needs. It could be pay, span of control, type of work, quantity of work, resources, culture, staffing, or any of a number of other items. It's best to have a well-defined sense of your "must haves" and "nice to haves" prior to heading into any interview, so you know how to assess whether or not it stacks up.

With opt outs, there is generally *some* flexibility, on *some* of these issues, *some* of the time. Few HR departments or hiring managers feel they have a perfect insight into the future, and there is an inevitable process of matching their desires for a new hire to the availability in the market. If something is a deal breaker for you, it's best to raise it early enough with your interviewer or recruiter so that both of you can determine if there's room for flexibility.

In sales, this is called "qualifying the lead." Here, we'll call it "chucking the dud." It's better to get duds out of your job search quickly and move on to greener pastures.

Twenty-five questions

To best understand company culture, the types of people who are successful there, and the particular requirements or desires for the position itself, I've assembled the following 25 questions for you to ask the HR person, the recruiter, the hiring manager, and the other people you interview. These are useful because they are open-ended enough for answers to be revealing, while relevant enough in context to be sensible. They don't feel threatening to ask — they allow you to feel sharp — and yet they can produce reams and reams of insight into the heart of the operation and its people.

With that, here are your 25 easy-to-ask, revealing-to-answer questions to take to an interview:

1. What's the biggest change your group has gone through in the last year? Is the strong economy growing your business? How much longer do you anticipate the economy to be strong for your company?
2. Which competitor worries you the most?
3. If I get the job, how do I earn a perfect score on my performance review? What are the key

accomplishments you'd like to see in this role over the next year?

4. What are the three things I can contribute in the first 100 days to make you feel great about hiring me? What are the most important things to the success of this role overall?

5. What's your (or my future boss's) leadership style?

6. How does sales / operations / technology / marketing / finance work around here? (i.e., groups other than the one you're interviewing for).

7. What type of people are successful here? What type of people are not?

8. What's one thing that's key to this company's success that somebody from outside the company wouldn't know about?

9. How did you get your start in this industry? Why do you stay? (Asked well — i.e., asking the question and then not interrupting at all — this question alone can have your interviewer chatting away for 10 or 20 minutes of fond reminisces.)

10. What are your group's best and worst working relationships with other groups in the company? What are the pain points you have to deal with day-to-day?

11. What keeps you up at night? What's your biggest worry these days?

12. Who are my customers (internal or external) and how do they measure me / us? Who views me (my team) as a customer (internal or external)?

13. Who are the heroes at your company? What characteristics do the people who are most celebrated have in common with each other? Conversely, what are the characteristics that are common to the promising people you hired, but who then flamed out and failed or left? As I'm considering whether or not I'd be successful here, how should I think about the experiences of the heroes and of the flame-outs?

14. The economy is strong, unemployment is down, and there's a lot of hiring demand out there. Among all the roles that you could have prioritized, why did you decide to prioritize this one instead of the others you could have hired for?

15. What is your reward system? Is it a star system / team-oriented / equity-based / bonus-based / pat-on-the-back-based? Why is that your reward system? What do you hope to get out of it, and what actually happens when you put it into practice? What are the positives and negatives of your reward system? If you could change any one thing, what would it be?

16. What does success for this group / team / company look like in one year? In five years?

17. What information is shared with the employees (revenues, costs, operating metrics)? Is this an "open book" shop, or do you play it closer to the vest? How is information shared? How do I get access to the information I need to be successful in this job?

18. Looking ahead, if we are going to have a very successful year in 2021, what will that look like? What will we have done in the time before then to make it successful? How does this position help achieve those goals? (This question helps show your ability to look beyond today's duties to the future more than a year away.)

19. How does the company / my future boss do performance reviews? How do I make the most of the performance review process to ensure that I'm doing the best I can for the company?

20. What is the rhythm to the work around here? Is there a time of year that it's "all hands on deck" and we're pulling all-nighters, or is it pretty consistent throughout the year? How about during the week / month? Is it pretty evenly spread throughout the week / month, or are there crunch days?

21. What type of industry / functional / skills-based experience and background are you looking for in the person who will fill this position? What would the "perfect" candidate look like? How do you

assess my experience in comparison? What gaps do you see?

22. What is your (or my future boss's) hiring philosophy? Is it "hire the attitude / teach the skills" or are you primarily looking to add people with domain expertise first and foremost?

23. Is this a new position, or an existing position? If new, why was it created and what are the expectations? If an existing position, where did the prior person go? What were the things that person did really well, that you hope to see in the next person? What are the things you hope will change?

24. In my career, I've primarily enjoyed working with big / small / growing / independent / private / public / family-run companies. If that's the case, how successful will I be at your firm?

25. What's the timeline for making a decision on this position? When should I get back in touch with you?

This list of questions enables you to come to (every) interview with a few good questions. Even though I'm usually the final person to meet a candidate here at Ladders, I'm always surprised when people I'm interviewing say they don't have any questions for me. Sure, it's understandable that you've already met four of my colleagues and they've answered a lot of the open questions you had about Ladders, but, really? You have absolutely no good questions for me? Not even just asking me the exact same ones to see if our answers vary? It's common enough, though, that it seems three interviews in one day is about as long as a candidate can maintain their ability to ask questions.

It's also a shame, because asking questions in interviews is only 50 percent about addressing your needs, explaining the role to you, and satisfying your curiosity. The other 50 percent of asking questions is showing your capability for critical thinking about the company, the industry, and the role. Using your question time to show off your good noodle by asking (brief) insightful questions, is a much better use of the time than saying that you have no questions. And even if you do run out of questions, there is the great, all-purpose, anytime, anyplace question to ask: "Is there anything else I should've asked but didn't?"

The Visual Interview

In 2020, the investment that your prospective employers are making in the employee experience is often a good indicator of how they feel about their employees in general. Your physical environment will have a tremendous impact on your productivity and happiness over the course of your years at a firm. Ensuring that you are mentally and emotionally prepared for the trade-offs is smart interviewing and good for your peace of mind. So do a

"Visual Interview" of your prospective employer's office environment.

You've perhaps mapped out the commute to this new potential office in your head, but have you also stepped through the very end of that commute several times? In the future, you'll be a regular, not a guest. And you'll be arriving at rush hour, or so, not before or after work. Are the parking and traffic flow in the mornings smooth and untroubled? Or does your arrival time for work mean that you'll be waiting to make a left turn into the company parking lot for 15 minutes every morning? Will you need to plan on a 10 minute wait for elevators because of the morning rush?

How is seating arranged at the office, and what's the overall office layout? How are desks and offices arranged? How much space, light, and quiet is each employee provided? How does that work with your style?

People are adaptable, so perhaps you can get used to it, but perhaps you can't. If you find it crushing to work in a status-driven hierarchical environment where the corner office is held out as the reward for years of experience, you should pay attention accordingly. Likewise, if the tumult of an open floor plan feels like chaos instead of productivity to you, you should choose wisely.

I'm flummoxed at the number of times people overlook this. Professionals go through multiple rounds of interviews at the hot new start-up, bemused by the informality of the meetings and the seating areas used for interviews, only to show up on the first day expecting that their office with a door, a desk, and a desktop must be hiding away for them somewhere. If you feel these factors greatly impact your ability to perform at your professional level, invest the time to determine suitability.

When you visit the office, what are people wearing? Are flip-flops optional? Is the dress code wearing a clean t-shirt and shorts? Button-down and jeans? Or is it a coat and tie kind of place?

How are meetings run, and can you observe them? What do meeting rooms reveal about the work culture at a prospective employer? You're likely to walk past a number of conference and meeting rooms during your visit to a company's offices, so what clues can you pick up in the process? Are the conference rooms packed? Are the people in the meetings mostly tuned in or tuned out? Is work being done in these meetings and are they filled with whiteboards and creativity? Or is it more of a lecture-from-a-Powerpoint style?

What's the food and beverage on offer? When they ask if you'd like a coffee or a water, take them up on the offer and get it yourself. This gives you an opportunity to visit the cafe or pantry or break room. Is it large and well-stocked, with a wide variety available? Or is it messy and tiny? Are they scrimping on supplies and offerings? Or is it a Google-esque cornucopia of snacks, bars, drinks, and menu options?

This can be a financially meaningful perk, by the way. If you are not buying breakfast, lunch or dinner with your own post-tax dollars over the course of 200+ days, that means thousands of incremental dollars in your own pocket. Great generals quip that "an army marches on its stomach." Does your future employer agree?

Similarly, I've heard it claimed that a trip to the bathroom is the best way to figure out how a company feels about its employees. Because the bathroom is invisible to the outside world, but something employees use every day, investments here show a conscious effort to improve the daily routine.

Are the bathrooms dingy, dimly-lit, depressing dungeons? Have the walls been painted since the 1970s? Or are they clean, well-stocked and well maintained? For this employer, how discretionary is employee happiness when nature calls?

These cues help give you a fuller picture of life at the new company. You can read too much into them, of course, and no office is a perfect slice of heaven. But it does help to ensure that your new environment is acceptable to you and will enable you to perform your best. So on your in-person interviews, in addition to asking questions, make sure you take some time for looking around and completing a Visual Interview.

Compensation

Save the money talk for last. You should have three ideas about compensation clear in your mind: what's realistically at the upper end of your range, an amount you'd accept, and a pay level you'd decline. You should write these down for your own reference early in the process, before the heat of salary negotiations begins to warp your expectations in ways you might not expect.

As mentioned earlier, it is becoming increasingly illegal in the United States for employers to ask for current salary, which creates an interesting dynamic that is to your advantage. Ideally, you'd like your future employer to reveal their number first. If it's your high-end number, you could take the offer right away. If it's below your low-end, you can reject out of hand. And if it's around your attractive number you may very well consider moving or staying as the situation suits you.

Should they ask, "What are your salary expectations?" you don't need to answer the question and shouldn't. Instead, you should get a range from the recruiter or HR person before going in: "In the interest of saving everyone's time, I would need to know what range this position is budgeted for before considering." Side-step any attempt to grill you about your current compensation with a Jennifer Anniston impression: "My understanding is that we're talking about a position at your company, and what my skills and talents would be worth in that regard, not what I've been paid in the past for a different role, with different responsibilities, at a different company — am I correct in assuming that or am I off-base?" Don't bring it up in interviews until **after** they know how excited they are about working with you, because that's when they're most likely to get excited about paying you more.

Be warned that experienced recruiters can usually get you to crack. Using pregnant pauses, social engineering and peer pressure, they often ask something like, "Having carefully considered your career and future, what are your salary expectations and why?" Without willpower, and practice at negotiating in high stakes situations, most candidates give up the requested information here. Try not to, even if they guilt you for it.

You might use evasive techniques such as saying: "Oh, I know that question, asking what my current salary is, was being phased out for a reason", or "Are you sure we're allowed to talk about that?", or "Oh, I'm paid fine, but I'm open to jobs that pay more, what's this one pay?", or "I'm canvassing the market to see what rates are."

When you get the number from them, hold it tight. You can decide later what you want to do with it. If you don't tell them what your current number is, it can only go up. Sometimes by a lot. But the key is to not share any of your confidential information prematurely (or ever, to be honest). You can always come back with your counter-offer later.

When it comes to compensation negotiations, try to get everything on the table at once — benefits, perks, pay, retirement, vacation, meals, car, etc. Let them know that you very methodically want to compare job duties and perks between all outstanding offers.

Throughout the process, when asked, it's best to indicate you are considering other roles, most or all of which are similar to the present one in most respects, and leave it at that. If some of them are very far afield, in wildly different industries or cities, do not share that with your interviewers, as these data points can confuse. Why, they might ask, are you interviewing for this job? Is it for fun, out of curiosity, or because you're actually interested in filling my role, right now? For now, it's sufficient to indicate that there are alternatives and demur on the specificity.

It's also best for you to communicate that you **want** the job, should the pay, conditions, and work be right for you. That leaves a ton of wiggle room, but also keeps the company interested. Displaying ambivalence about the role, or uncertainty about your interest, is never the best way to negotiate the most attractive offer. Ideally, you're able to convey a blazing enthusiasm for all things about your prospective employer with the only remaining issue being the tiny matter of pay. If they can get that detail out of the way, you are ready to jump in and get going.

When it's no longer true that you're interested in the job, it's best to be explicit and let the company know. The road is long and professional courtesy does pay off.

Gold star

In fifteen years of being the most widely-read career advice author in the U.S., the single best tip I've given, that has provided success for thousands of readers, is this:

When it gets to that part of the interview with your future boss where they ask, "Well, do you have any questions for me?" say yes, and ask…

"How do I help you get a gold star on your review next year?"

This bit of advice has helped more people in more interviews than any other bit of advice I've shared in the last decade-and-a-half that I've been writing on interviews.

Why?

Well, the interview process lends itself to self-absorption. You spend so much of the time talking about yourself that you risk sounding like one of those people who talks only about themselves.

Or, you might fall into the trap of becoming a "job analysis engineer" — asking all sorts of questions about the job and reporting structure and how it fits in with the company's five-year plan and so on — and risk missing the human connection with people you'll be working with. You can get so focused about the details of the job that you forget about the work.

Working together and being a good addition to the team means being concerned with how you are making the team successful. And that means being concerned with how well you are helping your boss succeed.

Asking this question shows that you have empathy. It shows that you have an interest in your boss's career and future success. It shows that you are not just a self-absorbed "what's-in-it-for-me" kind of person. And it shows that you know you are there to "give" as much as you are there to "get."

Thousands of professionals like you have told me how the interviewer's face lights up when asked this question. I have heard time and time and time again from our millions of readers how effective it's been in interviews.

(And, remember, you want the vibe to be a cool & relaxed Channing Tatum, not a cringing Jonah Hill.)

The gold star question is an easy tip to implement in your interviews: it's easy to do, easy to understand, and it's easy to measure. And from those who have used it, it's proved an easy way to create positive momentum in hiring conversations.

And that makes it the best bit of career advice I've shared in my career.

On your way out of the interview, make sure you have what you need — names, notes, email addresses, and a commitment to follow up, ideally with a date in mind. Use your time in the car or waiting for the train to jot down everything you know — better to be realistic and focus five or ten minutes of your time right now, than hope you'll do it an hour from now.

5. AFTER THE INTERVIEW: SAYING THANK YOU

Use your "thank you" to remind your interviewers of what they liked best about you. It's a chance to reiterate your interest and re-confirm the details of your ability to deliver on the job's three most important success factors. And it's a chance to outline the questions or concerns that you need addressed.

With your notes in hand from your day of interviews, review how it all went. Were the three most important things consistent across everyone with whom you spoke? Were their questions consistently on topic and directed toward hiring the same role? Were their answers to your questions consistent? Where did their answers vary? What did you learn about the role that makes you more excited? Less excited? Did you get a clearer sense of what they are looking for, and what they're not? Did they get a clearer sense of your priorities?

Your thank you note is a chance to frame your conversations and pull the company's hiring decision in your favor. It can't kindle a fire, but you can fan the flames a little in the direction you want to go. The length, tone, and formality should follow your industry practice, but the typical thank you note in American business practice for

2020 should be two paragraphs. People won't read much more than that.

Thank each interviewer again and reiterate, very briefly, how you can contribute. You want to demonstrate active listening by specifically referring to something you discussed in your interview, ideally in one half of a sentence. And your note should address two or three of the key factors, reminding your interviewer of your capabilities and experience in that area. Across all of your thank you notes, you should vary content, order, and coverage a little bit. Mix up sentence and word order and use slightly different phrasings so that, should your emails be passed around to others, it won't look like you simply copied and pasted.

As a matter of fact, do not copy and paste. It's easier and takes less effort to copy and paste, and that's exactly why you shouldn't want to. Show your interviewers that you care enough and respect them enough to write an individual note. Do not use a template. And it is really much, much better if you retype by hand each of your emails to each separate person you met. Copy-and-paste edits too often show up at your recipient's inbox with font sizes varying word to word, with spacing and sentences broken up and looking awkward. It can even be the case that the email that looks great when you send it to yourself will look awful when it arrives in another person's corporate inbox. At

Ladders we send over one billion emails per year, and we've experienced firsthand how frustrating this can be. Nonetheless, the plain fact is that, relative to the time you've spent interviewing, and the importance of this follow up, the risk of having the formatting go very wrong is not worth it. Retype all your thank you emails by hand.

It's also worth mentioning that some formal environments still welcome the handwritten thank you note, though very few expect it. Perhaps 2 percent of candidates for professional jobs ever write handwritten notes. Handwritten notes do not change the outcome one way or the other, but may add lift and momentum to your candidacy. Formalities are increasingly unexpected, and in some cases, unwelcome, in U.S. business circles. You'll have to judge your industry's expectations accordingly.

I'd like to say that you shouldn't have to take the customs around "thank you's" too seriously, because it can seem silly. But the plain fact is that in some cases, your interviewers take it very seriously, and the content of your thank you emails can set the tone for the outcome of the entire interview process. It's easiest to do these notes well if you maintain the discipline of writing notes either during or immediately after each interview. You'll certainly never remember the specific comments later: "I enjoyed our conversation about changes in the mobile ecosystem, and how my background could be useful in designing the advertising strategy for Wakanda's new tourism campaign." This helps the interviewer remember why they liked you when the time comes to make a decision.

Interviewing is stressful, and I know there's a temptation to spend the time you're waiting to hear back fretting anxiously. There are endless worries and recriminations you can generate for yourself. But you really need to separate your emotions from an effective assessment of your performance. It's extraordinary how often I'll hear from readers who thought they'd done very poorly in an interview, only to have an offer come through along with feedback that the interviewers loved that person. It's natural to feel anxious, but don't let that cloud your judgment.

Thank you

Speaking of "thank you"s, I'd like to **thank you** for spending your time and attention with me and this little book for the past 90 minutes.

We started off with me bombing an interview at the start of my career, and have progressed through all the areas I should have thought about in advance and for which I could have been better prepared.

We introduced the notion that interviews are uniquely strange occurrences in modern life. Nothing in our past prepares us for the stress and discomfort of being subjected to the persistent and direct questioning of strangers for hours on end. The anxiety we may feel comes from our "fight or flight" response to stressful situations, and is a normal, expected, universal reaction to the modern interview.

We reviewed the goals of interviewing — to provide an accurate picture to employers of our capabilities; to obtain an accurate view of their opportunity; to determine if there's a good fit between the role and our experience; and to generate a good job offer for ourselves when there is.

We hammered home the efficacy of asking for the three most important success criteria for any job. Having these three factors in mind, we're able to structure our interviews, our answers, and our questions around the needs of our future boss or employer, rather than our own needs. And by speaking to our future boss's requirements, we made our candidacy more attractive than alternative candidates who did not.

We reviewed preparing your mind, your body, your research, and your reasons for interviewing. By taking care of your physical needs, and being mindful of the difficulties imposed by unfamiliar environments, we removed unexpected or unwanted surprises of hunger, thirst or discomfort from intruding on your interview. By reviewing the right amount to research opportunities and interviewers, we've reduced your anxiety about your level of preparation, and also prevented the excesses of overdoing it. And we've encouraged you to consider, mindfully, once again, your purposes for interviewing — a person with a plan is powerful, and so long as you know why you're interviewing, the sky's the limit for your future.

We reviewed how and why companies are hiring in 2020. It's a very strong economy, but unfortunately, company managers' interviewing skills are still a bit rusty and can be haphazard. The current trend in interviewing is toward the behavioral interview and we reviewed seven categories of questions, with seven questions each, in great depth. We also covered what great answers and bad answers to those behavioral interview questions sound like. We completed our discussion of company interviews with how to handle specialty interviews and illegal questions.

We turned to questions that you can ask in your interviews, and we discussed the essential importance of active listening. We studied 25 detailed questions you can ask in any interview, including the extraordinarily powerful 'Gold Star' question. And we discussed how you might best handle the crucial topic of compensation.

My poor performance two decades ago came from being unprepared, poorly rested, hungover, without any idea of the company, role, or people I'd be interviewing. In retrospect, it's amazing I made it in the door! But it's a cautionary tale with a purpose and a positive outcome.

By following the advice in this book, I hope you'll have better conversations, less anxiety, more insights, and improved outcomes in your own interviews. The stakes are high, but the topic is one with which you are very familiar. With the proper amount of preparation, you will be able to do terrifically well in your own interviews and continue your upward progress in your career.

I hope it's been as enjoyable for you to read this book over the last 90 minutes as it has been for me to write it. Good luck with all your interviews and with your inevitable career success...

I'm rooting for you!

MORE BEST PRACTICES & ADVICE ONLINE

For free information, behavioral questions, and tools to help with your interviews, visit:

www.theladders.com/career-advice/interviews-guide

Find us on Twitter:

@LaddersHQ

ABOUT THE AUTHOR

Marc Cenedella is Founder and CEO of Ladders, Inc., the home for $100K+ careers.

He is the author of the largest career advice newsletter in the United States, which reaches an audience of nearly 10 million weekly. His best-selling careers guides, *Ladders Resume Guide, Ladders Interviews Guide*, and *Ladders Job Search Guide*, each of which reached #1 on Amazon's Career Bestseller list, are top resources for professionals of all levels to improve their job search.

A nationally renowned thought leader on careers, career management and recruiting, Marc is frequently sought out by national media organizations for his expert commentary on employment and entrepreneurialism.

He has been profiled in The New York Times, Wall Street Journal, Fortune, Wired, and Businessweek, appeared on CNN, Fox News, MSNBC, CNBC, and Bloomberg and has spoken at Ignition, SHRM, and Internet Summit as well as Harvard Business School, Columbia University, and Yale.

From Fredonia, New York, Marc holds an MBA with High Distinction from Harvard Business School, where he was named a Baker Scholar, as well as a B.A. in Political Science from Yale College.

Notes

Notes

Made in the USA
Middletown, DE
15 February 2020

84828191R00076